I've seen the extraordinary impact of Mac's work in key global cities; particularly during our time spent in New York City. This book tells the story of mutual friends who are having tremendous impact for Christ.

Keith Getty, Getty Music

Mac has gathered powerful testimonies of generosity from around the world. This is a must-read for anyone seeking to steward well all that God has entrusted to them.

David Wills, president emeritus,
National Christian Foundation

Much like his mentor Bob Buford did in his book *Finishing Well*, Mac has chosen well the stories of men and women whose humble response to God's prompting became a calling to live disruptively.

Greg Barnes, president and senior consultant,
Halftime Talent Solutions

A Disruptive Generosity is a compelling series of stories that ignites one's desire to give generously. An inspiring road map to experiencing the joy of giving.

Holt Lunsford, founder and chairman,
Holt Lunsford Holdings

Spiritual renewal is always followed by economic revitalization (Matthew 6:33). In his new book, Mac Pier reminds us of the powerful connection between philanthropy and gospel movements. A must-read for those who live at the intersection of faith and culture.

A. R. Bernard Sr, president/CEO, Christian Cultural Center/
Commission of Religious Leaders

Pier's decision to hold a magnifying glass over the generosity of a few will light an unquenchable fire of generosity in a countless multitude.

Julian Archer, founder, *Faith vs. Finance*

Stories are the currency of the day, and in his book *Disruptive Generosity*, Pier opens up a global treasure trove that shows the correlation of Kingdom movements and generous givers.

Daryl Heald, founder, Generosity Path

God is the Ultimate Giver, Jesus is the Ultimate Disruptor. He changed it all. Scripture says "The world of the generous gets larger and larger; the world of the stingy gets smaller and smaller" (Proverbs 11:24), and in Mac's book we come to a better understanding of God's call to us to live bigger lives and to be change agents, disruptors, in a world that cries out for change. God is inviting us to reflect his generosity toward us through our generosity toward him and others; our giving changes the world and is the great apologetic of today!

J. Todd Peterson, chairman, Pro Athletes Outreach;
NFL kicker, 1993–2005; chairman emeritus, Seed Company

Mac Pier keeps strong company! Mac has introduced us to obedient co-laborers who will sharpen the iron in our own lives to yield rich fruit.

Katherine Barnhart, The GROVE Group

Using biblical truths from Isaiah, Mac Pier shows how modern-day leaders demonstrate the faithfulness of God in their disruptive generosity. God is indeed the Great Choreographer using our modern-day generosity to fulfill his ancient promises.

Michal Powell, Dallas community leader

A DISRUPTIVE GENEROSITY

STORIES OF TRANSFORMING
CITIES THROUGH
STRATEGIC GIVING

MAC PIER

BakerBooks
a division of Baker Publishing Group
Grand Rapids, Michigan

Published by Baker Books
a division of Baker Publishing Group
PO Box 6287, Grand Rapids, MI 49516-6287
www.bakerbooks.com

Printed in the United States of America

Library of Congress Cataloging-in-Publication Data is on file at the Library of Congress, Washington, DC.

ISBN 9780801075650
ISBN 9780801077777 (cloth special edition)

17 18 19 20 21 22 23   7 6 5 4 3 2 1

In keeping with biblical principles of creation stewardship, Baker Publishing Group advocates the responsible use of our natural resources. As a member of the Green Press Initiative, our company uses recycled paper when possible. The text paper of this book is composed in part of post-consumer waste.

I dedicate this book to leaders who have shaped my own generosity.

Billy Graham, who challenged Marya and me to go anywhere in the world God would send us at the Urbana '79 Student Missions Conference.

Desmond Tutu and John Perkins, who challenged me to be radical in my love for the entire body of Christ.

Bob Buford, who has been so disruptively generous and helped me launch the New York City Leadership Center in 2008.

Contents

Acknowledgments

I want to extend my appreciation to Brian Thomasson and the Baker team for their enormous efforts to complete this book. They have been very generous toward me.

I also want to thank Dan Balow and Tina Jacobson for their guidance.

Many thanks to all the friends who made time to share their stories with me. My hope is that this book tells them well.

Thanks to our board and staff at the New York City Leadership Center who work hard to catalyze gospel movements around the world.

Thanks to my brother Rick who allowed me to use his home for extended weeks to write and edit the manuscript in the "house on the hill."

Thank you to my immediate family: Marya, Anna, Lucas, Jordan, Christine, Kirsten, and Basanth, who have been a part of this journey in New York City for more than thirty years.

Special thanks to Noah and Layla for the joy they bring to a grandfather with the aspiration that they grow into a life of generosity.

Foreword

Mac Pier is one of the most effective leaders in the world. I mean those words literally. Whether measured against presidents or prime ministers, generals or multinational CEOs, megachurch pastors or global parachurch leaders, his gifting, passion, and results are absolutely unique and globally transformative.

It has been my personal privilege to know and work with Mac across many years in many settings. I have seen him encourage leaders over private lunches in Dallas and heard him speak to thousands of leaders from around the world in New York City. I have spent multiplied hours with him in personal conversation and public gatherings.

I have never known a leader as gifted as Mac at gathering the body of Christ and inspiring them to greatness. I have never seen a leader as passionate about reaching every nation with the good news of God's love. He is a visionary with the courage of Peter, a scholar with the mind of Paul, an encourager with the spirit of Barnabas, and a Christ-follower with the passion of John.

Quite frankly, I know of no one like him.

It is therefore a great personal privilege for me to commend A Disruptive Generosity to you. This is Mac at his finest. He begins with his own story, recounting thirty years in New York City after moving to the city with his pregnant wife, Marya, with nowhere to live. Over these years, he has seen the evangelical population grow by 500 percent in Manhattan. Hundreds of churches have been planted and thousands of leaders have been catalyzed into God's mission for the city. From the beginning, Mac recognized the intimate link between generosity and mission. As he notes, "a unique dimension of money is that it can use the temporal to impact the eternal." In *A Disruptive Generosity*, he interviews forty leaders representing ten countries. They tell their firsthand stories of how God disrupted their lives through philanthropy. I know many of these leaders personally and can attest to the accuracy of Mac's accounts and the transformation they have experienced.

The best way to read Mac's book is to follow his suggestion: read one story a day. Reflect on the passage from Isaiah connected with that story. Then pray for God to use your generosity to disrupt the world with the gospel.

As you walk this journey, you will discover three timeless and transforming truths.

One: God "causes nations and nature to rejoice in him." As you interact with these leaders, you will be drawn closer to their Lord and the joy he reserves for those who follow him fully. You'll discover that, as Mac observes, "God takes an act of obedience, and the seeds of that obedience bear fruit generations later." That's the greatness of our Lord. He uses us in ways we cannot imagine or predict. As Alfred North Whitehead noted, great people plant trees they'll never sit under.

Two: What God has done, he can still do. Mac tells us the story of the Lausanne Congress in 1974, one of the most significant gatherings of Christians since the Jerusalem Council in Acts 15. He takes us to Movement Day with Tim Keller in

New York City seven years ago, the spark that lit fires of collaboration and kingdom advance in cities around the world.

Then he introduces us to people like Mart Green, the son of the founder of Hobby Lobby. Mart has set out to see that people speaking every one of the 6,500 spoken languages in the world would have a Bible in their language. Just as the Spirit spoke to the Pentecost crowds in their languages (Acts 2:6), he is doing the same through leaders like Mart.

Three: God works through people in gospel relationships. Mac tells us about "a movement of friendship" whereby the Lord connected him with the leaders you'll meet. He is right: every image of the church is collective—a vine with many branches, a body with many members. We are the body of Christ, the visible representative of our invisible Lord. Jesus works through each of us as we work with all of us.

Why would the Holy Spirit move Mac to write *A Disruptive Generosity* now?

Christianity is growing in unprecedented numbers around the world. If current trends continue, the People's Republic of China will soon be the largest Christian nation on earth. The population of Brazil will soon be one-half evangelical. The population of South Korea is already one-third Christian. More Muslims are coming to Christ than ever before in Christian history, many after seeing dreams and visions of Jesus.

Now God wants us to join this global awakening through our intercession, witness, and generosity. Never has there been a better time in Christian history for us to invest sacrificially in the worldwide advance of the kingdom.

Beyond that, Christianity is facing unprecedented opposition in the Western world. Growing numbers of people see our faith as outdated if not dangerous. With the shifting tides of morality in our day, many evangelical Christians are branded as prejudiced and marginalized as irrelevant. Never has there been a more urgent time in Christian history for us to engage sacrificially with God's people in advancing the gospel into our dark culture.

Mother Teresa was once opening an orphanage in a global city. A press conference ensued. A skeptical reporter shouted at her the question, "How will you measure the success of this?" The tiny Albanian nun turned into the glare of the camera, smiled, and said, "I don't believe our Lord ever spoke of success. He spoke only of faithfulness in love."

In *A Disruptive Generosity,* you will meet leaders whose faithfulness in love is touching the nations and changing the world. If you make their definition of success yours, you will join them.

You cannot measure the eternal significance of present faithfulness.

Dr. Jim Denison

Introduction

"Come now, let us settle the matter," says the LORD. "Though your sins are like scarlet, they shall be as white as snow; though they are red as crimson, they shall be like wool."

Isaiah 1:18

On March 20, 2008, I spoke at my father's funeral in Avon, South Dakota. That afternoon I was standing in our family bank lobby, looking at the portraits of the three generations of Piers who had gone before me. They reminded me of that moment in the film *Dead Poets Society* when John Keating, played by Robin Williams, has his students look at the photos of students who had gone before them. He challenged them with "*Carpe diem*"—"Seize the day." We have only one life.

My great-grandfather, Tom Pier, started the bank in 1914. He had a sixth-grade education and two friends who added their ten thousand dollars to his five thousand dollars. The Community Bank is now more than a century old. As I reflected on those photographs of my great-grandfather Tom, I realized how much I am like him. He took great economic risks to pursue a dream. He was willing to have his life disrupted.

My wife, Marya, and I left South Dakota in 1984 with a van full of possessions and moved to New York City. Marya was three months pregnant with our oldest daughter, Anna. We had no place to live. All we had was a call from God and some important assurances from my InterVarsity supervisor, Janet Balajthy, that we would make the plan work. Looking back over the past thirty years, I see one truth that has been proven over and over: *Every risk we have taken for God has been transcended by his provision.*

My family's bank has beautifully served its rural community for five generations. The risk Tom Pier took in 1914 has made the lives of thousands of others better. Farms have been sustained, educations have been resourced, and personal lives have been improved.

In the past thirty years, we have seen enormous change in New York City both spiritually and socially. In twenty-five years we have seen God grow evangelical Christianity in Manhattan by 500 percent. We saw the violent crime rate drop by 70 percent in the five years from 1995 to 2000. We have seen hundreds of churches planted, ministries incubated, and thousands of leaders catalyzed. It's been a thrill to be an eyewitness to this as well as a modest contributor.

Why This Book?

Having grown up in a banking family and been a career missionary, I have always been fascinated by the relationship between mission and generosity. The 2013 book *Gospel Patrons* by John Rinehart is a brilliant read on the relationship between philanthropy and profound global spiritual movements in history.

One of the unique dimensions of money is that it can use the temporal to make an impact on the eternal. *A Disruptive Generosity* is a modest, modern-day version of *Gospel Patrons*. Conversations with Ray Nixon from Dallas have greatly stimulated my thinking in this direction, and for this book I have interviewed forty leaders from ten countries. They told me their stories of how God has been disruptive through their philanthropy.

At this writing, our small organization, New York City Leadership Center, has had its best two years from a fundraising perspective, in 2015 and 2016. We've raised $9 million over two years. Six years ago, we were raising closer to $1 million per year. This is not a lot of funding in the grand scheme of things, but more important is that it has allowed us to convene leaders in 2016 from ninety-five nations for Movement Day Global Cities, assist Redeemer City to City with planting new churches, and train thousands of nonprofit leaders in New York City.

Personally, Marya and I have focused our generosity on our church, our sponsorship of twenty World Vision children, and our participation in Movement Day Scholarships. Our church in New York City is nestled among one hundred language groups we want to see impacted. We began to sponsor World Vision children in 1982 and see World Vision as perhaps the best way to catalyze resources to alleviate global poverty. I have met these children and have seen that each sponsorship impacts sixty others in the community. I have taken two hundred leaders on World Vision trips who have in turn sponsored nearly eleven thousand children. Movement Day catalyzes leaders to make a difference in their cities.

We have also used our home as a source of generosity. The year that Kirsten was born, we hosted three hundred people in our home, including a hundred overnight guests. In our thirty years in New York City we have provided long-term housing for women from Guyana, Trinidad, and Hungary.

How to Read This Book

I am weaving together three big ideas in this book. The first is God's vision for the world as referenced in the book of Isaiah. Isaiah gives us the big picture of a God who comes to transform cities, who causes nations and nature to rejoice in him. Isaiah announces the coming of a Savior who will be the ultimate expression of the generosity of God in the gospel.

The second is that of movement. A spiritual movement is taking place when the Christian population is growing faster than the general population. A movement is taking place when the church is making an impact on the great social realities of a city or nation. A movement is taking place when Christian leaders are finding themselves in places of cultural influence.

I reference two specific gatherings that have catalyzed movements. The Lausanne Congress held in 1974 was hosted by Billy Graham and John Stott. Those men were perhaps the two most significant "movement makers" of the twentieth century in the church. Lausanne gathered Christian leaders from every country in the world to ask how we as the church could bring the whole gospel to the whole world.

The second gathering is Movement Day, cofounded by Tim Keller and me in 2010 in New York City. In the past seven years, we have hosted fourteen thousand leaders from four hundred cities and ninety-five nations. Leaders gather to study, to train, and to strategically plan how to advance the gospel in their own cities.

The third big idea is that of a relational network, a movement of friendship. The forty leaders I interviewed for this book all have amazing stories. More importantly, they have become friends and have generously been willing to tell their stories. These relationships are less than ten years old, and we have a deep sense of acceleration taking place.

You will notice a small group of key relationships in this book:

Doug Birdsall was the executive director of Lausanne for the Cape Town Congress in 2010. Nearly a third of the interviews in this book are connected back to Lausanne and to Doug. This book is also a short history of the Lausanne movement and how God is using it. Movement Day has become the expression of Lausanne's work in cities around the world.

Bob Doll and I met at that Cape Town congress, and our relationship developed rapidly. Bob joined our board in 2014 and became our board chair in 2015. His involvement has attracted many other high-capacity Christian marketplace leaders. Bob, Tim Keller, and I proposed the idea of a "three-legged stool" to reach a city: a marketplace leader, a pastor, and a ministry agency leader.

Ram Gidoomal is the chair of the Lausanne Committee. Ram's networking capacity is unparalleled. He has connected me to many leaders across Asia, Europe, and Africa. Many of their stories are captured here.

What you will see in this book is what I call a "relational tree." You can trace much of its content to Billy Graham and the 1974 Lausanne Congress. One of the important truths in this story is that God takes an act of obedience and causes the seeds of that obedience to bear fruit generations later.

A Final Encouragement

The promise of Isaiah 1:18 is that God will remove our sins and make them as white as wool and as clean as snow. The crimson of Jesus's blood would remove the sins of the world for all who trust in him and believe the gospel. This book purposes to tell how Jesus is using the disruptive generosity of ordinary men and women to tell the story of the Great Disruption. Jesus is the ultimate disruptor.

Let me challenge you to take a few minutes every day for thirty-one days to read one chapter, reflect on the passage from Isaiah, and then pray that God will use your generosity to disrupt the world with the gospel. He may show you an idea to develop, a truth to memorize, or a person with whom you can connect.

Carpe diem. God will always transcend your risks with his provision.

A PRAYER

Jesus, thank you for disrupting the world in your coming. Take the loaves and fishes of our resources— time, talent, and treasure—to disrupt the world to experience the transformation from scarlet sins to souls white as wool. Amen.

1

Boldness

HOW RAY AND DENISE NIXON SAID YES TO GOD'S CALL

> Then I heard the voice of the Lord saying, "Whom shall I send? And who will go for us?" And I said, "Here am I. Send me!"
>
> Isaiah 6:8

When Isaiah received a vision of the Lord, high and lifted in his infinite holiness, Isaiah's only response was, "Woe to me! I am a man of unclean lips" (Isa. 6:5). The Lord cleansed Isaiah and asked him, "Who will go for us?" Isaiah's response was, "Send me!" (v. 8).

Isaiah's voice was influential, given that he served under four kings. The unique platform he enjoyed was because of his national prophetic role. We cannot underestimate the importance of being placed in a strategic vocation and location.

Perhaps no word better embodies the life and ministry of Ray and Denise Nixon than *boldness*. They have courageously raised their hands to give of themselves again and again. What has given their leadership additional significance is their engagement with the financial industry, life in Dallas, and participation with a globally strategic church.

At a recent donor gathering for Movement Day Global Cities, Ray spoke to the attendees. Ray challenged the attendees to be bold and to have a vision for Christ. He challenged those present to risk it all.

Ray and his wife, Denise, have never lacked a God-sized vision for the city they've been called to serve.

In 2014 I met Denise through a mutual friend, Abigail Powell. Denise introduced me to Ray later that year over dinner. I quickly learned he knew Dallas as well as any marketplace leader I had ever met knew his or her city. Since 1994 Ray has worked as executive director for Barrow, Hanley, Mewhinney & Strauss, LLC, a financial investment firm. The firm manages $100 billion. I interviewed him in March 2015 at his Dallas offices on Ross Avenue.

Denise is deeply involved with Bible Study Fellowship. Through her BSF experience, her heart was warmed toward Jesus in a fresh way. Ray began his own spiritual journey with daily spiritual practices. Ray told me, "I was finally converted to Christ at the age of forty-two. My encounter with him radically changed my life." As the result of this deepening spiritual life, the Nixons joined Park Cities Presbyterian Church in 2001.

A Bold Faith—Denise

Denise has always had a heart that leaned toward the poor, and her social work orientation has been informed by her deep sense of compassion. She told me, "In the 1980s I got to see a different side of Dallas. I saw the poor and underserved. I was involved in St. Luke's Closet, which provided clothing to the poor in our city."

As her involvement grew with Park Cities Presbyterian Church, she was invited to lead a women's retreat. Rather than conducting a traditional conference-center outing, she decided to take the women from this relatively affluent church on a field trip. They traveled to West Dallas—one of the poorest communities in the DFW metroplex. Denise's understanding of the underserved in West Dallas was central to the formation of Serve West Dallas.

Serve West Dallas is a remarkable organization that stands on the shoulders of the thirty-plus-year ministry of Pastor Arrvel Wilson and the work of West Dallas Community initiatives and several faith-based organizations. In 2007 a few West Dallas ministries approached Pastor Wilson, senior pastor of West Dallas Community Church, saying it would be hugely beneficial if the faith community could work closer together in West Dallas.

From then on, discussions about forming a faith-based collaborative began among West Dallas nonprofits, Christian organizations, community pastors, several Dallas businessmen, and several large suburban churches. This new partnership would function under the mantra "The whole is stronger than the individual parts," believing West Dallas could be transformed only if people started working together.

During the initial period of Denise's involvement with SWD, index crime rates dropped 49 percent, and the estimated saving of property resolution totaled more than $2 million, based on improved tax revenues, improved property values, reduced crime, and reduced maintenance cost.[1]

The power of the Serve West Dallas model is that it demonstrates with measurable impact what collaboration can achieve in a city. The vision is to see Serve West Dallas replicated in other impoverished Dallas communities. Denise understands that the poor need a bold voice on their behalf.

A Bold Faith—Ray

After Ray's conversion, he joined the board of the Salvation Army in Dallas. The Army began in 1865 under the leadership of William Booth. It has become one of the most globally recognized humanitarian agencies in the world. But in Dallas the Salvation Army had run into difficult times.

As Ray joined the board, he and his fellow board members began to turn the Dallas Salvation Army effort around. By the time Ray became the board chair, it had become the largest Salvation Army expression in the world. Its services include addiction recovery, helping families in crises, and running children's camps.

I attended the Salvation Army Christmas luncheon in December 2013, where President George W. Bush was the keynote speaker. That luncheon raised more than $2 million. Today the Salvation Army has eleven locations in the Dallas-Fort Worth metroplex and has developed anchor partnerships with AT&T and the Dallas Cowboys.

The beauty of Ray's involvement with the Salvation Army is that it meshes his and Denise's concern for the poor with their passion for evangelism. Ray has been the only Dallas leader to receive the prestigious "Others" award from the Salvation Army for exemplary service to "others."

Coming to Christ later in life, Ray has a sense of fearlessness about his witness that is contagious. One outlet for Ray's bold witness is his yearly pilgrimage to Cuba. Every November he takes a group of men on a trip there with East-West Ministries. East-West was founded by John Maisel, a Purple

Heart recipient from the Vietnam War. John is a contagious evangelist who planted East-West to do evangelism and church planting globally.

On this annual trip to Cuba, men go door-to-door to share their faith with the help of a translator. Of the many involvements Ray has, this trip is perhaps the most invigorating of them all. He is a man of action.

Ray told me, "This annual trip to Cuba has been absolutely transformational for the men who come. Many of them are sharing their faith for the first time with someone else. I work every year to bring a new group of men because I know about the impact that this will have on them."

A Bold Faith—to the End

Denise and Ray have been instrumental from the early days of the development of Movement Day, but one of the statements Denise made to me on a recent call really inspired me. She said, "I am involved with Movement Day because I don't want to slide into home base at the end of my life. I want to leave it all on the field."[2]

Isaiah and a Willingness to Go

What has made the Nixons' work so effective is their radical availability into their sixties. Isaiah challenges us in our own sense of availability. Life is a vapor! Choices matter. How do we respond to God's question to Isaiah, "Whom will go for us and whom shall I send?"

The words of Isaiah 6 echo the challenge of Jesus in Matthew 28. Isaiah's words are a historic echo of a missionary God who challenges us to be fearlessly bold in our witness.

POINTS TO CONSIDER

1. God can remarkably use you, even if your conversion is later in life.
2. We need to reach out from our comfort zones to understand the needs of the less fortunate.
3. By bringing our own gifts and abilities to innovative ministry, to agencies like the Salvation Army and East-West Ministries, we maximize their effectiveness.
4. Investing in fellowship with believers who are ethnically and denominationally different is critical. Doing so is a high-leverage, high-impact strategy.

A PRAYER

Jesus, help me to be a risk taker. I don't want to slide into home base at the end of my life. Use me to share Christ boldly, to serve compassionately, and to motivate my peers to do the same. Amen.

2

Bound Together

HOW TERRY DOUGLASS AND DOUG BIRDSALL'S FRIENDSHIP REVIVED LAUSANNE

> Foreigners who bind themselves to the LORD to minister to him, to love the name of the LORD, and to be his servants, all who keep the Sabbath without desecrating it and who hold fast to my covenant— these I will bring to my holy mountain and give them joy in my house of prayer.
>
> Isaiah 56:6–7

Isaiah had a vision of seeing people from all over the world come to meet with the Lord and with one another. The Lausanne movement is a modern-day manifestation of that vision. The vision of Isaiah and the passion of Jesus were to see the radical inclusion of those normally excluded from the community of God. In Isaiah's day, it was the foreigner and the eunuch who were excluded. Jesus turned the merchants' tables upside down in the temple to protest their exclusionary money-lending practices.

The Lausanne movement brought the global evangelical church together in a radical act of inclusivity. It has been a modern-day Pentecost of leaders from every tribe and nation gathering to worship the Lord.

Lausanne Revived

Billy Graham and John Stott had a vision to unite the global evangelical church. The expression of that vision came together in 1974 at the Lausanne Congress in Lausanne, Switzerland, with leaders from hundreds of countries. On August 1, 1974, the Lausanne Covenant, authored by John Stott, was published. The introduction to the covenant states

> We, members of the Church of Jesus Christ, from more than 150 nations, participants in the International Congress on World Evangelization at Lausanne, praise God for his great salvation and rejoice in the fellowship he has given us with himself and with each other. We are deeply stirred by what God is doing in our day, moved to penitence by our failures and challenged by the unfinished task of evangelization. We believe the Gospel is God's good news for the whole world, and we are determined by his grace to obey Christ's commission to proclaim it to all mankind and to make disciples of every nation. We desire, therefore, to affirm our faith and our resolve, and to make public our covenant.[1]

In the ensuing years, working groups were formed, Young Leader Gatherings were held, and momentum was created for global partnership. The next Lausanne Congress took place fifteen years later in 1989 in Manila. Then Lausanne hit a lull. More than two decades passed before the Third Lausanne Congress, Cape Town 2010.

A Friendship between Two Men

Doug Birdsall became a missionary with Asian Access in 1980 after graduating from Wheaton College and Gordon-Conwell Theological Seminary. Doug stepped into the role as executive chair for the Lausanne movement in 2004. Doug's vision was to revive the Lausanne movement by convening a third global congress. Doug expressed to me that one of the most critical friendships in the journey toward Cape Town 2010 was his relationship with Terry Douglass.

Terry Douglass grew up in a middle-class family in western Tennessee as one of seven children. He says, "I was a normal kind of kid who loved sports, liked science, math, and building things." Terry was also affected when the Atomic Energy Commission visited his high school. The AEC provided encouragement to write his senior paper, "Atoms for Peace." He graduated from high school in Jackson, Tennessee, in 1960, and was motivated to study engineering at the University of Tennessee. At the time engineers were earning one hundred dollars a week, which felt like a lot of money to him.[2]

Terry finished his PhD in 1968, doing research and writing his dissertation on the coincidence time measurement for positron emitters. He began to work on PET technology—positron emission tomography as a diagnostic tool for cancer. We know this as the PET scan. By 1976 the ability to commercialize PET scan technology came about, and by 1983 Terry had built a business called CTI Molecular Imaging, which has as its mission "To make Clinical PET a reality." Congress gave authorization in the FDA Modernization Act of 1997 to make this technology available to the broader medical community.

In early 2005 the company went public and was sold to Siemens for $1 billion on May 20. Terry and Doug were traveling together on an Asian Access trip. Terry had to call a board meeting from Japan with his cell phone to transact the sale of the company on Thursday night. On Friday morning the sale was publicly announced on the stock market.

Immediately after the sale of the company, Doug and Terry were on a plane to Beijing. Doug asked Terry, "What are you planning to do with the rest of your life now that you have sold the company?" Terry responded, "I haven't thought about it."

Doug told him he had accepted the position of chairman of the Lausanne Congress for World Evangelization, and that there would be a third Congress in 2010. Terry said, "Tell me what I need to do to help." Terry would travel with Doug around the globe in the coming years to pursue the vision of a Cape Town Congress. In February 2007 the two men traveled to Cape Town, South Africa. The purpose of the trip was to decide on the host city for the Third Lausanne Congress on World Evangelization.

During their final meeting in Cape Town, Michael Cassidy, founder of African Enterprise, said, "It seems right to the Holy Spirit and to us that the Third Lausanne Congress should be held in Cape Town in 2010."

Later that same day Doug asked Terry if he would provide a lead gift to launch the preparations for the Cape Town Lausanne Congress. Terry responded, "Of course," and he provided $1.5 million. Terry said later, "I got chills seeing where this was going and, looking back, recognizing that 4,200 leaders came from two hundred nations."

Ongoing Ministry

Terry describes his life's journey in three phases: developing the PET scan, helping launch Lausanne 2010 in Cape Town, and developing proton therapy. Proton therapy is a medical treatment that allows a more targeted cancer treatment. He says, "We are building world-class cancer treatment centers in Knoxville, Nashville, Orlando, and other cities in the USA and around the world."

Terry's ongoing work has allowed him to create Provision Foundation. The foci of their work is currently in the United States, China, Guatemala, and Haiti. Extensive work has also been done to reach at-risk children and international students attending universities in the United States.

Even though Terry graduated from high school nearly sixty years ago, he says, "I have heard if we remain healthy, that our most productive decade is in our sixties and our second most productive decade is in our seventies. The Bible doesn't say anything about retiring. I am a big believer in Ephesians 2:10, which says, 'For we are God's handiwork, created in Christ Jesus to do good works, which God prepared in advance for us to do.' I want to be able to stand before the Lord and hear him say, 'Well done, good and faithful servant.'"[3]

Isaiah and Calling

Through Isaiah, the Lord said those who hold fast to his covenant will have joy. We have an opportunity in our later years to apply our experience to our generosity. As we grow older, we should have a sharper sense of what our unique Ephesians 2:10 calling is all about. We want to apply our generosity to our unique calling. Terry and Doug were bound together in friendship. We are bound to the Lord in our affection and generosity to him.

POINTS TO CONSIDER

1. God can use the vocational awakening in even a young boy to create a future global platform.

2. God providentially brings people into our lives at specific moments to create opportunities we would never have imagined on our own.

3. Don't discount what God may do in the latter years of your ministry. You may have your greatest impact in your sixties and seventies.

A PRAYER

Jesus, awaken in each of us your plan to weave our vocational abilities with lifelong friendships to reach the world. Help us to envision what you can do in us through the later decades of our lives. Amen.

3

Game Changer

HOW BOB AND LESLIE DOLL DISCOVERED THEIR NEXT CHAPTER

> I will give him a portion among the great, and he will divide the spoils with the strong, because he poured out his life unto death, and was numbered with the transgressors. For he bore the sin of many, and made intercession for the transgressors.
>
> Isaiah 53:12

Isaiah's vision of Jesus in chapter 53 is perhaps the most important in all the Old Testament. Jesus is not only portrayed in his suffering and execution; he is portrayed as the Great Intercessor over all of us as transgressors. Chapter 53 describes Isaiah's future vision of the coming of Jesus in Christ's redemptive act. The death of Jesus on the cross is the ultimate, game-changing fact of human history.

Bob Doll and I met (along with Tim Keller) for the first time in Cape Town, during the Lausanne Congress in October 2010.

Bob and his wife, Leslie, had been lead investors in the Cape Town Congress, along with Terry Douglass.

Bob was the chief equity strategist for BlackRock investments at the time, managing one of the largest portfolios in the world. He is one of the most highly respected investment managers on the globe. His top-ten annual predictions are published around the world every December, and he is regularly featured on CNBC and interviewed by the *Wall Street Journal*. Priyan Fernando, formerly of American Express, said, "Bob Doll is the final word on global markets."[1]

I met Leslie a few months later when the couple agreed to partner with Tim Keller and me in the New York City Movement Project. The NYCMP was a five-year initiative that saw the successful planting of sixty NYC area churches, trained twenty-six thousand Christian leaders, and hosted fourteen thousand leaders from four hundred cities for Movement Day. The Dolls were the investors "first in" on the project, with a one million–dollar pledge.

The Dolls have come to their place of radical generosity through a combination of increased awareness of needs in the world, opportunities through collaboration, and at times through receiving personal challenge. When considering a contribution to the Cape Town Congress, they thought they would give one hundred thousand dollars. They were challenged to add a zero, which they did.

Molded by Crises

Leslie grew up in Dallas, Texas, where her dad was a financial analyst and her mom was a stay-at-home mother. Her family members were faithful churchgoers, and she remembers making a confession of faith while attending a Christian camp, Pine Cove, at the age of seven.

When she was twelve, her parents divorced. During our interview, Leslie commented, "My parents' divorce deeply shook my sense of security. My mom was now divorced with three children to raise, no income, and no vision for the future. With a keen sense of adventure and a passion for the world, I concluded I would have to make my life work and not depend on anyone else. I earned my MBA at SMU with a plan to go into international business."

Bob's crisis happened later in life, while he was working for BlackRock. In 2012 he felt led to retire from BlackRock after being confronted on issues related to his faith. He had been interviewed at several conferences and talked about the central role his faith played in his life. The interviews were circulated on the internet and he met with resistance from leaders at his company. He says, "I really struggled after my departure from BlackRock. I realized how much my identity had come from my work."

Bob reflected on his journey in between his position at Black-Rock and his next assignment at Nuveen. "I was moping around the house one Saturday morning about my job loss, when Leslie asked me to count the number of emails I had received from friends concerned for me. The number was in the hundreds. That gave me perspective on how God might want to use my next chapter."

The Dolls journeyed through the Halftime Institute by Bob Buford together in the 2011 to 2012 time frame. That experience shaped their sense of specific calling as a couple. Thus, Bob developed a personal mission statement:

> I will, with God's help, maintain and enhance a global platform and voice through my ability to manage money and speak about financial markets, so that I can use both money and a Christian worldview to impact and serve organizations and Christian business groups at the convergence of faith and work to

enable ministry and increase commitment to Christian faith in life and work.

Leslie's Journey with the Middle East

Bob and Leslie were married in 1987 and started a family in 1990. Leslie says, "With Bob's career and raising a young family, I had to put some of my aspirations on hold. It was not until my children were becoming independent that I could consider the fullness of God's purpose in my life and pursue the passions he had given me of engaging the world, particularly the Middle East."

Over the past few years, Leslie has made five trips to the Middle East each year. She has worked closest with Strategic Resource Group in its commitment to the Great Commission there. In addition, Leslie has been meeting with, and serving as an advocate for, persecuted Christians in the region. The dreams she had and the plans she made to go into international business are now being fulfilled by God. He has called her to his divine international business.

I asked Leslie to comment on the most important things global Christians need to understand about God's activity in the region. She said, "God is causing an increase in dreams and visions of Jesus among the refugees. One man in Iraq told us that ISIS captured him and sixteen family members and put them in prison. That night his father had a dream that Jesus came to him and said, 'Do not be afraid.' He convinced his family and two hundred other people held in the same prison to pray that Jesus would rescue them. In the morning, with no explanation, ISIS leaders let all two hundred go free.

"One pastor in Iraq told us that in the ten years before the refugee crisis he had met only two Yazidis with whom he shared the gospel. One trusted Christ, and the other did not. As a result of ISIS brutality, the Yazidis have had to run for their lives and have relocated near the Christians. The pastor said he has thousands of them in his backyard and could now share Christ with two thousand Yazidis a day!

"In Lebanon, we met with veiled Muslim women from Syria attending prayer meetings and praying together for God's protection over each other's loved ones who were missing or kidnapped at the hand of the Syrian regime in ISIS. It was remarkable to hear them thanking God for making them refugees so that they could discover life in Jesus! We are hearing and seeing videos of pastors baptizing Syrian and Iraqi refugees with plastic pools and buckets of water used to wash dishes. One church in Beirut had four hundred members a year ago. Now it reports over twelve hundred—75 percent of whom are Syrian refugees. What a time for harvest!"[2]

While Leslie has focused on the Middle East, Bob joined Tim Keller and me as the "third leg" of the city gospel movement "stool." The three legs in our methodology are pastor, mission leader, and marketplace leader, working together to make an impact on a city. Bob's credibility as a senior businessman has been extraordinary.

Bob's Journey with the New York City Leadership Center

From 2010 to 2016, as Bob became more involved with us at the New York City Leadership Center, our organization has grown 400 percent. His credibility has drawn other senior marketplace leaders to be involved strategically and philanthropically. He now serves as our New York City Leadership Center board chair.

Bob has said, "I participate on a dozen boards, but no where do I see the Holy Spirit working as powerfully as within NYCLC and Movement Day." He has marveled at the speed of growth of Movement Day to involve leaders from ninety-five nations within six years. He sees it as a natural extension from the Cape Town gathering in 2010.

Bob and Leslie's pastor, Matt Ristuccia, is also a board member for the New York City Leadership Center. The congregation of Stone Hill Church has been deeply involved as well.

Bob has been a regular presenter at Movement Day as a plenary speaker and track content provider. His message to his peer marketplace leaders is clear and compelling. He outlines these principles:

1. Jesus spent more time talking about money and possession than any other subject.
2. Don't store up wealth on earth (Matt. 6:19).
3. You can't take it with you; send your wealth ahead (Randy Alcorn, *The Treasure Principle*).
4. Earth is not our home, and everything we have God gave us.

Personal Giving and Prayer

The Dolls describe their giving in three tiers:

1. They give a lot to a few places when they deeply believe in the mission, the kingdom impact of their investment, and they are deeply involved.
2. They give substantially to a variety of ministries in whose mission they believe.
3. They give smaller amounts to several other Christians in secular charities.

They confess, "As a married couple we do struggle with our giving priorities. Bob prefers to be involved in multiple causes. Leslie is more convinced of a focused regional mind-set."

Their call as senior marketplace leaders is to have this perspective: "Billy Graham has said that marketplace Christians are to the gospel in this century what medical missionaries were to the gospel in the last century. When marketplace leaders are involved with a cause, the speed of [spreading] the gospel accelerates. We are living in a unique time in history. God's timing is perfect and he is preparing opportunities for us to be significant."

Critical to these opportunities is reliance on God through prayer. Leslie commented, "Prayer really is making a difference in the Middle East. After my fifth trip to Iraq in two years, I was reflecting on experiencing the devastation of the diabolical destruction by ISIS on the Christian village of Qaraqosh. For the past thirteen hundred years, the greatest prayer meeting in all the world has been taking place. Muslims have been praying five times a day. This really is a spiritual battle that will only be won by the prayers of God's people and his work through the body of Christ."[3]

Isaiah and Intercession

Jesus is portrayed in Isaiah 53 as one making intercession for the transgressors. We are invited into this high priestly privilege as those who pray to Jesus and with Jesus as intercessors for a desperately broken world. Jesus is relentlessly praying for the world. Will we join him?

POINTS TO CONSIDER

1. God can use the crises of your life to shape you for deeper faith and greater fruitfulness.

2. Marketplace leaders are the most strategically placed persons to be game changers for the gospel. How is your own marketplace role affected by your commitment to Christ?
3. Radical generosity involves not just philanthropy, but physical presence.
4. Christians need to be informed, engaged, and willing to sacrifice for persecuted brothers and sisters in the Middle East.

A PRAYER

Jesus, awaken your church to the possibilities of a game-changing opportunity in the great global cities of the world. In particular use your church to enter into the suffering of your people in the Middle East. Amen.

4

Glory

HOW RAM AND SUNITA GIDOOMAL
TOOK A STAND FOR CHRIST

> The glory of the LORD will be revealed, and all
> people will see it together. For the mouth of the
> LORD has spoken.
>
> Isaiah 40:5

The glory of the Lord is never revealed more powerfully than
when people discover him from diverse world religions. Isaiah
wrote throughout the latter half of his book about nations coming to discover the Lord. The Gidoomal story is the journey of
two Hindu families coming into an experience with the Christ
of Isaiah's vision.

I saw Ram in London in May 2014, during our first planning
meetings for Movement Day Global Cities. He graciously invited
me to his home, where we had dinner. We were together with
his wife, Sunita, the following week in Lausanne for fortieth

anniversary celebrations for the initial Lausanne Congress in 1974. In October 2014 Ram was passing through New York City the day after our Movement Day that year. He joined us for meetings. Providence was at work.

India Disrupted

Ram was born in Kenya after his family had been forced to flee during the 1947 partition of India, and lived in Mombasa till he was seventeen years old. The family were traders of silk imported from Japan. After Kenya's independence the Gidoomal family relocated to London in 1967. They were forced to leave everything behind in Kenya.

Ram's father had died at an early age, and he was raised by his mother and uncles. After moving to London, the fifteen family members squeezed into a four-bedroom flat. They began a corner shop that multiplied across London.

Ram's family were practicing Hindus. He describes his mother as quite superstitious in her expression of Hinduism. In England, the family remained both culturally and religiously Hindu and were large donors to many local Hindu temples.

While attending university, Ram was introduced to Christianity by a fellow student who was with Campus Crusade. Ram struggled with the Four Spiritual Laws and the challenge they represented. After significant wrestling with the truth of Christianity, Ram responded to the gospel and converted. Ram says Patrick Johnstone, author of *Operation World*, was so stunned when meeting with him that he had to sit down. He said Ram was one of only fifty people in his entire tribe of millions of Sindhi Hindus who had ever converted to Christianity.

Ram describes the reaction of his Hindu family to his conversion. "My family was shocked. My mom said that you can change your passport but you can't change your religion. She thought my conversion would be like a toothache and that it would go away."

Sunita's family had immigrated to London earlier. She was raised as a Hindu, but she knew about Christianity through school. Sunita became familiar with the Bible and attended the local Anglican church for one year. She and Ram were married in 1976.

Sunita describes her conversion to Christianity in 1978, during her time in Geneva while Ram was working there. She says, "I saw the reality of Christianity in people who were extremely helpful to me. They helped me in many practical ways. They accepted Ram and me as internationals away from home. I attended Bible studies with women, and Christianity became real to me."

Slumdog Millionaire

Ram was deeply affected after visiting India in the 1980s. About seeing the film *Slumdog Millionaire*, he says, "That movie was an accurate portrayal of the lives of many people who lived in the massive slums of India. I felt like I had to do something disruptive about this following my visit to that same slum in 1987."

He retired from his family company by 1991 and began to work on social entrepreneur efforts to alleviate poverty in India. One of the initiatives was called Christmas Cracker. Its objective was to identify missionaries for the twenty-first century.

The concept of Christmas Cracker was to allow young people to run initiatives like restaurants on local streets, local radio stations, local newspapers, and fair trade shops—for a month. Over the course of the program, from 1988 to 1995, $10 million was raised. The funds were then distributed to agencies like World Vision and Tearfund for poverty programs not only in India but across the globe. Each year had a different theme, such as wells, street children, or child prostitution.

The genius of the program is that it served third-world food at posh Western prices. It had two hundred restaurants at its peak, and millions of dollars were raised each year. It also identified emerging missionaries with a heart to serve the poor entrepreneurially.

Running for Mayor of London

In the late 1990s, Ram was challenged to run for mayor of London. A group of young activists from the Movement for Christian Democracy in the United Kingdom came to Ram and Sunita and said, "We are looking for a credible candidate to run for mayor of London; would you have any suggestions?" Ram gave them several names, but a little while later they came back to him and said, "We would like you to stand—the committee is unamimous." Ram agreed, and so was born the Christian Peoples Alliance, a political party that seeks to demonstrate Christian values in the public square.

Ram was also influenced by the opportunity to win one of the twenty-five seats in the newly formed Greater London Assembly based on proportional representation. He said, "If I could run and get sixty to seventy thousand votes, I would get more than 4 percent of the vote and earn a seat for the Christian Peoples Party."

Ram ran for mayor in the 2000 and 2004 election cycles, and his candidacy raised $400,000 from people many of whom were not Christian. Ram describes the platform the Christian Peoples Alliance ran on:

Social justice

Compassion

Respect for life

Reconciliation

Empowerment

Stewardship of resources

In each election, Ram secured just under one hundred thousand first- and second-preference votes. The platform was so persuasive that the prime minister and opposition party leadership started campaigning for the Christian vote with vigor in subsequent elections across the United Kingdom.

Sunita says, "Administrating the campaign for eight years was all-consuming. We were working to launch the party nationally. Ram would speak in all kinds of churches and to the media at all hours of the day and night."

When I traveled to London in April 2015, I saw the influence Ram had with churches. Whether it was Holy Trinity Brompton, All Souls Church, or faith leaders, they all conveyed enormous respect for Ram and Sunita's courage to have Ram run for mayor of London.

Movement Day United Kingdom

Ram and Sunita have been instrumental in building a team to work with Roger Sutton from Gather (Evangelical Alliance) to host Movement Day United Kingdom. Ram and Roger hosted a planning team in December 2015 to create a path to a gathering of Christians across the United Kingdom and Europe. The group is meeting at Central Methodist Hall in Parliament Square, the mother church of Charles Wesley, in October 2017. It has a two-thousand-seat auditorium.

When asked why they believe in Movement Day, Ram responded, "Movement Day brings together pastors, marketplace leaders, and missionaries to impact the same city. This is a tremendous way to impact every significant city around the world."[1]

Isaiah and the Glory of the Lord

Isaiah saw a day when God would bring honor to himself by bringing the nations of the world to global cities. How remarkable that God would use an Indian couple from a Hindu background to raise up a global witness from the world's leading global city, London, England.

POINTS TO CONSIDER

1. God is using political unrest and migration to create a witness to himself.
2. God honors the consistent and persistent witness of his people.
3. Christian leaders need to show courage to become role models in the public square of politics.

A PRAYER

Jesus, use your church to witness to the world in cities. Be honored by the courage of leaders to stand up for you in the public square. Amen.

5

illumiNations

MART GREEN FINDS A VISION
FOR BIBLES IN EVERY LANGUAGE

Nations will come to your light, and kings to the brightness of your dawn.

Isaiah 60:3

Toward the end of his book, Isaiah wrote of a compelling vision he had. He saw a time when nations and kings would gather and be drawn to the supremacy of God in the person of Christ. In his commentary *The Prophecy of Isaiah*, Alec Motyer describes the final ten chapters of the book of Isaiah as the coming of the Anointed Conqueror. As Christ comes in the fulfillment of this Isaiah prophecy, the nations and their rulers will be drawn to pay homage to the King.

What needs to happen between modern-day global spiritual reality and this future picture? Nations and leaders need to be illuminated to the incarnate Word of God by the written Word of God.

The Hobby Lobby and Mardel Stories

Mart Green and I had breakfast together in Manhattan on December 4, 2016, at the New York Luncheonette on 50th Street. We talked about the dream to see God disrupt the world by every person in the world having access to the Scriptures in their own language. It somehow seemed appropriate to be having this discussion in a city where over eight hundred languages are spoken.[1]

Mart's grandparents were preachers who wanted all six of their children to be preachers. They all were, except one: Mart's dad, David. Mart says, "My dad felt like a second-class citizen as a businessman. Then God spoke to him and told him he was called and anointed to be a businessman. In 1970 he started Greco Frames, a manufacturing company. Then in 1972 he opened the first three-hundred-square-foot Hobby Lobby store. Today there are more than 750 Hobby Lobby stores in the United States."

As a teenager, Mart left college to begin Mardel Christian and Education bookstores in 1981. Mardel has grown to thirty-five stores in the southwestern United States with twelve thousand titles. Besides books, Mart bought and sold Bibles, developing a real passion for empowering others with the Scriptures. That passion also included donating to Bible translation causes.

He was invited to the dedication of a new translation of the Bible into a foreign language on February 7, 1998, in Guatemala. Mart saw the power of someone encountering the Scripture in their own language for the first time. He describes his experience with Gasper, who lives in Guatemala with the Eastern Jacaltec people, on February 7, 1998.

"I got to the dedication; and it was a big ceremony that went through town, and they all had a parade. There were four Eastern Jacaltec people that helped translate the Bible over a forty-year period. One of those who had been there the entire forty years was Gaspar. When Gaspar went forward to get his Bible, because they gave it to him during the ceremony, he did something I'd never seen before. He openly wept."

After reflecting on that experience, Mart realized that although he owned multiple Christian bookstores and dozens of Bibles, he had never spent consistent time in Scripture on his own. As I pondered this story, I sensed Mart was experiencing two simultaneous, profound epiphanies—the personal need to be as moved as Gaspar at the opportunity to engage God's Word, and to experience the holy discontent of so many people in the world having to wait so long to have the Scriptures in their own language.

Mart describes that epiphany. "That same year I had this impression of the head and the heart. Something I felt like the Lord put on me that was going to happen in the future. That doesn't happen to me very often. I just felt like this is going to happen someday. It was going to be a project so big that no ministry partners could do it alone. Both ministry and resource partners would have to come together with other ministries."

A Bible-Engagement Movement

Mart's vision is to see the Bible translated in every one of the six thousand languages spoken on the globe. In 2006, eight years after his 1998 epiphany, he met Bobby Gruenewald. Gruenewald would create YouVersion, the Bible application for the iPhone. It had extraordinary success with eighty-three thousand Bibles downloaded over the first weekend the app went live. Mart says, "God was doing something amazing. It was actually changing how people were engaging with the Bible."

Mart and Gruenewald began to extrapolate the challenge of getting all the necessary permissions to create a global digital library of all existing Scriptures. Green called a meeting of the Bible translation community in May 2010, including Wycliffe, American Bible Society, Biblica, Seed Company, and the Summer Institute of Linguistics. He challenged the group, "What would happen if we could build one standard digital Bible library? We wouldn't have to chase the rights to translated Scriptures. I would like to challenge us to finalize an all-access goal so that everyone in the world could have at least some Scripture in their own language by 2033."

This challenge gave birth to Every Tribe Every Nation (ETEN), a fabulous collaborative group of partners committed to the same vision. The core group meets every month to review progress and update on strategy against the end goal.

Seed Company had a donor gathering in 2014 titled illumiNations to celebrate the one thousandth translation of Scripture. Three hundred people attended. He says, "I was stunned by the program. I saw the event raise $21 million over the three-day weekend."

There Mart met Todd Peterson, the mastermind behind illumiNations, for the first time. He shared with Mart that he wanted illumiNations to be a movement to financially resource the ETEN efforts. This movement would attract investors from around the world committed to the 2033 vision: 95 percent of the world having a full Bible, 99.9 percent having a New Testament, and 100 percent having at least twenty-five chapters of the Bible. Imagine that Scripture could be translated into forty-five hundred languages in less than twenty years, though it has been translated in only two thousand languages in the last twenty centuries. This vision has the similar power of the Gutenberg Press upon the Reformation five hundred years ago.[2] Concurrent with the momentum of illumiNations is the Museum of the Bible led by Steve Green, Mart's brother. The museum will launch in November 2017 in Washington, DC, as the culmination of a 1.2 billion–dollar effort from the global faith-based community. One of the areas in the museum will be dedicated to illumiNations. The vision is to see three thousand churches and leaders each adopt one of the global languages.[3]

A Discussion in a New York City Diner

When we met, Mart and I spoke about all the ways God was at work. We talked about the twin realities: an urgent need to capture everyone's language for Scripture translation and a simultaneous phenomenon that the world is now showing up in our large cities at the rate of three million new people every week. The planet's population will grow 20 percent in twenty years, to nine billion people. What is God up to? We agreed that this was an important conversation to see where these two opportunities converge.

Isaiah and the Illumination of God

Isaiah had a vision of the kings of the earth being attracted to the glory of God. This would be realized in the magi coming to Bethlehem. All over the world God is connecting leaders in high places to God's people through God's Word.

The work of the Green family and their partners is the most robust effort perhaps in church history to bring about this illumination. Like Mart Green, we need to start with an examination of our engagement with the Word of God.

I took up the challenge in July 2014 to read the Bible every ninety days, cover to cover. I also read daily from *A Guide to Prayer for All God's People* by Rueben P. Job and Norman Shawchuck, and from Tim Keller's devotional *The Songs of Jesus*, which takes one through the Psalms in one year. I have found the more rooted I am in the Word of God, the more I see the work of God unfolding all around me in technicolor.

POINTS TO CONSIDER

1. The potential impact of any partnership is exponentially greater than when leaders and agencies are working on their own.
2. The enormity of the unmet task requires an urgent level of partnership and humility.
3. God wants to speak to every person in his or her own language and to have an intimate relationship with that person.

A PRAYER

Jesus, we invite you to come and illuminate the hearts of every person on the planet. Give a sense of urgency and a spirit of agreement across the global church to achieve this grand objective for your name's sake. Amen.

6

Light

SANTOSH AND BHAWNA SHETTY PLANT NEW CHURCHES IN INDIA

> It is too small a thing for you to be my servant to restore the tribes of Jacob and bring back those of Israel I have kept. I will also make you a light for the Gentiles, that my salvation may reach to the ends of the earth.
>
> Isaiah 49:6

The final half of Isaiah's book pulses with the passion of God to see the nations come to know his salvation. No one is outside the scope of God's concern, not from any nation or world religion. God was always challenging Old Testament Israel to have concern for the widow, the orphan, and the foreigner.

As we live in a world where nearly one-third of its population is Chinese or Indian, God wants us to pay attention to his work among Chinese and Indian people all over the world.

The Chinese church is the fastest-growing church in history. The Indian church is producing unusually gifted and generous leaders, like Santosh and Bhawna Shetty.

I met Santosh in Singapore in September 2014 through our mutual friend Daryl Heald. Santosh and his wife, Bhawna, who live in Dubai with their four children, come from Hindu backgrounds. Santosh commutes to India every week to run his company, Expat Group. Expat Group concentrates on land development and commercial real-estate development. The company has an annual revenue of $85 million and 450 employees.

I have been privileged to stay with the Shetty family in Dubai and to visit their church there. Santosh also provided a travel stipend to the 150 leaders who came from India and Sri Lanka to attend Movement Day Global Cities.

The Journey to Christ

In our interview, Santosh described his spiritual journey. "My family moved to Dubai from India in 1980. My two sisters were attending an American college in Cyprus in 1986. They were befriended by other college students who were Christian. They were convinced that Christianity was true. When they returned to Dubai, my mother was upset. Mom's response was tempered over time when she saw how remarkably transformed my sisters had become. My sisters were more patient and gracious than they had ever been before. Eventually one of my sisters worked with Youth With a Mission for six months."

Santosh made a commitment to Christ in 1990 through the influence of his sisters. He went back to college in Mumbai, and graduated in 1993, having studied economics, marketing, and business management. One of his primary mentors was

Shelton Davidson, a Mumbai pastor who also started the Mumbai Transformation Network.

Immediately after college, Santosh met Bhawna through common friends in Dubai. Bhawna was the oldest of four siblings. Santosh influenced Bhawna to follow Christ in 1994 before they were married in 1995. Bhawna is from the same Hindu tribe as Ram Gidoomal (see chapter 4).

She describes her conversion. "I had been attending a Bible study led by an American. On my final day of work, I put out a fleece before God that I needed to finish a transaction for someone who was traveling. Supernaturally the transaction was worked out. I saw that God was real and active in people's everyday lives. This led me to put my trust in Christ."

Radical Generosity

The Shettys have a profound grasp of the magnificence of their spiritual life in Christ. That realization has translated into their personal philanthropy. Santosh told me, "Whenever Bhawna would see money accumulating in our bank account, she became disturbed. She is so aware of so many great needs that we are always working to give away as much as we possibly can."

In 2000, when Santosh's company was small, he made a commitment to give away 90 percent of his income. In the next fifteen years, the company would grow from $500,000 in value to more than $150 million in value. Santosh says, "I realized that the 10 percent I was living on in 2015 was more than the 90 percent I was living on in 2000. Bhawna and I have decided to live on a small percentage of my income. We don't see any other way of living."

I asked Santosh about the causes for which he is particularly passionate. India has nearly three times more Hindus than

America has Americans, and he is quite taken by the Disciple-ship Movement in India. The effort is in collaboration with the Timothy Initiative and FMF.

We also talked about Movement Day's impact on India. Santosh attended the gathering in New York City in October 2016. He said, "I see Movement Day's primary contribution as bringing unity among leaders of different spheres. The alliances that come out of Movement Day are extraordinary. You cannot shape a culture without leveraging the influence of a company in a city. Movement Day removes the fragmentation of a city and results in heightened impact. I see the potential impact of Movement Day across the great cities of India and our four hundred million people who live in those cities."[1]

Isaiah and Light

Isaiah saw a day when people from all backgrounds would come to discover the truth of God in the Messiah. God's salvation is extending to the ends of the earth in part because of the extravagant generosity of God's people.

POINTS TO CONSIDER

1. God is reaching people who have had very little under-standing of Jesus for centuries.
2. Radical salvation should translate into radical generosity.
3. One generous person can be a pivotal point for a com-munity, city, or nation.
4. Generosity is measured as much by what we keep as what we give.

A PRAYER

Jesus, thank you for drawing the nations to yourself. Connect your church worldwide to reach parts of the world like India, where so many billions of people need you. Amen.

7

Salvation

WHY ADAM WALACH
WANTS TO SEE EUROPE TRANSFORMED

Surely God is my salvation, I will trust and not be afraid.

Isaiah 12:2

Throughout his long career as a national prophet, Isaiah must have had moments when he felt alone. He witnessed national and spiritual turbulence over several decades. He had many reasons to be afraid—political coups, spiritual apostasy by the nation, and threats to his own life.

Yet Isaiah knew the work of God transcended his lifetime. He was anchored in the belief that God was the ultimate Rescuer, the ultimate Savior—his Savior.

Adam Walach has had a transformative experience of the salvation of God from an Eastern European context. He has seen how a nation can be transformed politically and spiritually in one lifetime.

I was introduced to Adam in 2014 through mutual friends Bob Doll and Ram Gidoomal. Over the past three years, I have been impressed with his intention to help build a collaboration among givers and kingdom investors for the re-evangelization of Europe.

Growing Up in a Communist Context

Adam has Polish roots, although he grew up with his brothers in what was then called Czechoslovakia. He describes his growing up. "I came from an ordinary family. We had our first television when I was thirteen years old. I had three older brothers, and the oldest was a great example. My parents came from a Lutheran background, and we are now Brethren. I invited Jesus into my life in 1984 during an evangelical camp while we were still living under communism."

When we spoke, Adam commented on his own spiritual growth. "Even though I had made an initial commitment to Christ, I did not grow during my university years. I drifted spiritually. It was not until I met my wife, Grazyna, that I began to take my spiritual life more seriously."

Adam described a time of nonviolent transition of power in Czechoslovakia called the Velvet—or Gentle—Revolution, which took place from November 17 to December 29, 1989.

Achieving Success

Adam began a company with his two brothers in 1990 from scratch, after the fall of communism in his part of the world. The company started an imports/exports business and soon crystalized into two main fields: pharmaceutical and nonalcoholic beverages. For the next decade their company, Walmark, was wildly successful, becoming the number-one company in juices in the Czech Republic and Slovakia, and number one in vitamins and food supplements in Central and Eastern Europe.

In 2013 the company sales exceeded $100 million in US currency and had eight hundred employees. In 2010 Adam and his two brothers received the Ernst and Young Entrepreneur of the Year Award 2010 in the Czech Republic.

Despite the tremendous growth of the company, Adam was restless. He says, "I felt like I was living in the world from 1990 to 1999. When I met Grazyna, my life took a new direction. I felt like I was coming home. In 2006 I made a radical decision. I rededicated my life to God. I spent the next two years studying part-time in an online Bible school with my wife. I became an active member of the church with a desire to serve God 100 percent. I determined to give away more than 50 percent of our personal income."

Adam comments further on the journey. "In 2012 we sold 50 percent of the company and created significant liquidity for kingdom purposes. I attended the Halftime Institute in 2014 and spent an eight-month sabbatical with my family in the USA. I wanted to finalize my calling. By 2015 we sold 100 percent of the company."

Calling

Emerging from his sabbatical, Adam felt led to create the European Great Commission Collaboration. He concluded that one of the reasons Europe is presently so poorly evangelized is because evangelization efforts in Europe have "not been strategic, not collaborative, and not compatible."

Adam believes Europe exported secularism, humanism, atheism, communism, and existentialism to the rest of the world.

Now is the time to envision European and global Christians with an opportunity to grow Christianity across the continent. Adam's analysis of the trend of European Christianity is this: "Despite overwhelming history, track record, and presence, Christianity is arguably in free fall. Many people who are numbered as Christians have never heard the gospel. Despite many claiming some level of adherence to 'Christian Values,' few share their faith and few understand even its most basic principles. More than two-thirds of European Christians cannot name half of the Ten Commandments."

The rapid trend of secularization calls for targeted, well-resourced, thoughtful engagement and scaling of successful pilots. We are seeing the rapid expansion of Islam across Europe.

The vision is to "see a transformed Europe by people who come to Christ and are discipled in a local church." Their website describes the mission of the EGCC:

The European Great Commission Collaboration (EGCC) exists for the purpose of glorifying God through an alliance of like-minded global funders who believe that by working cooperatively they can more effectively resource Christianity in Europe.[1]

Adam is encouraged by the start of the effort. Initial meetings were held in 2015, followed by an EGCC Prague Summit in May 2016. He says, "The Summit was a great event and there were fifteen givers/kingdom investors as participants, plus sector leaders who presented us with the situation in Europe. We had wonderful and fruitful times sharing knowledge and experience in giving, getting to know about each other, and building relationships."[2]

The belief is that strategic leaders and partners can accelerate the impact across Europe together and that community leads to unity and unity leads to impact. The EGCC holds an annual donors' forum for fellowship and education about the current needs and strategic initiatives in Europe and for encouragement leading to collaboration.

Isaiah and God's Salvation

Isaiah pointed us toward a God who is our salvation. He also pointed us toward a God who puts us on mission to proclaim news of a Savior. Isaiah was telling the world about a coming Savior. Our assignment is to tell a world, including the world of Europe, about a great Savior.

POINTS TO CONSIDER

1. God is allowing marketplace leaders to be successful and then point them toward a larger kingdom opportunity.
2. Europe is a continent with a great spiritual history, yet it needs a coordinated and massive effort to address its great unmet spiritual and social needs.
3. Collaboration is the vehicle to give practical expression to the unity of the church in hard places like Europe.

A PRAYER

Jesus, you love Europe and directed Paul to plant the first church in Philippi. Speak supernaturally today into the hearts and minds of missionaries and philanthropists like Lydia, who can resource the work that is so urgently needed across that great continent. Amen.

8

Refuge

HOW PRAYER GUIDES KEITH CHUA'S GIVING

You have been a refuge for the poor, a refuge for
the needy in their distress, a shelter from the storm
and a shade from the heat.

Isaiah 25:4

Isaiah had a profound vision of God as a refuge. Given the enormous challenges of life for those who were poor and handicapped in his day, Isaiah saw God as a comfort. He described compassion or lack of compassion as a spiritual indicator for God's people, and he had a view of God as one who paid attention to the destitute.

Throughout his book, Isaiah drew the linkage between the spirituality of a people in prayer and their generosity of heart. I saw this incredible linkage in the story of the Chua family in Singapore.

I met Keith Chua in Manhattan on a Sunday night in 2014. Bob Doll was with us. Bob and Keith had met during their involvement with Lausanne. Keith, whose home is in Singapore, was traveling in the United States to see one of his children. We had a late dinner together that night, and Bob introduced the work of the NYC Movement Project and Movement Day.

Later I found myself twice in Singapore, in fall 2014 and summer 2015. Singapore is named by *Forbes* magazine as the fourth most influential city in the world. I was stunned by the vibrancy of the Singaporean church, including the strength of the Christian marketplace community.[1]

Another common link with Keith is the Haggai Institute. Haggai is a global leadership training movement active with Movement Day in recent years. Haggai was founded in 1969 and has trained nearly thirty thousand leaders. Keith chaired the Haggai Institute from 1994 to 2008 and participated in its training in 1987.

He currently serves as CEO of Alby Group and says, "For the past thirty years, I have divided my time evenly between my business responsibilities and my philanthropic efforts."

Revival in Singapore

Keith's family has roots in Penang, Malaysia. His father was born in Penang, and his mother was born in Singapore. His great-grandmother on his mother's side was one of the fortunate girls of her time—the late 1800s. Her father was forward-thinking and wanted his daughter to have an opportunity for education. She was one of the first Chinese females to receive a formal education, tutored by a Methodist missionary in Singapore.

The great-grandmother became a visible person in the community philanthropically, supporting educational causes. She owned land and transferred it to the Methodist Church in 1922, and a school was built on it.

After a clock tower was built on the campus of that school, students met to pray there in 1972 and 1973. Revival broke out, leading to a wave of conversions in Singapore in the 1970s. Keith was converted in 1973 through the influence of his brother, and then his parents were converted. Another brother had gone to Australia and was converted there. The family spiritual circle was complete when the great-grandmother became a Christian and was baptized at the age of ninety-six. The entire family had become Christian by 1975, and Keith's parents became very active in the church.

The revival of Christianity in Singapore continued and built up steam after the 1978 Billy Graham Crusade there. When we spoke, Keith commented, "The crusade resulted in the conversion of a number of first-generation Christians who were younger. They brought their parents to faith in Christ, and the movement became multigenerational. In the 1980s and 1990s, key marketplace leaders became Christian. This began a transformational impact."

Keith's father was a leading automobile distributor in Malaysia and Singapore. As Keith grew up, his parents took care to teach the value of money. He says, "We needed to value money appropriately. This was very helpful in shaping how I looked at issues and resources later in life."

Keith moved into the business world after finishing National University in Singapore. He took responsibility for his family investments, and very early in his career he became involved with the family's ownership of the Garden Hotel, which they owned from 1980 to 2009.

He says, "The hotel became a spiritual meeting place in the 1980s when Singapore was going through a time of spiritual renewal. It was a center of visitation for Christian leaders and was made available for hospitality. The hotel provided a critical place for networking among Christian leaders. The hotel also provided us with a way of making wealth to give it away."

Keith says his vocational calling is to create entrepreneurial businesses. He likes to see initiatives started in a number of diverse areas. These initiatives have provided employment for those less fortunate in the food and beverage industries.

Keith, with the National University of Singapore Business School, also initiated the establishment of Asia Center for Social Entrepreneurship and Philanthropy. The hope is that this will become a discipline of the business school. The vision is that this will become a research platform for strategic coordination of philanthropy.

Influences on Philanthropy

I asked Keith what some of the influences were in his philanthropic decision making, including his support of Movement Day. He commented, "I could see that Movement Day was rooted in the New York City prayer movement. That resonated with my own experience with Sharing Of Ministry Abroad since the early 1980s. SOMA teams traveled to promote spiritual renewal in the churches through prayer. I was involved with the founder, Michael Harper, and joined the SOMA International board in 1995. We took the SOMA conference internationally in 2000. We had the conference in Cape Town in 2000, which was the precursor to the Global Day of Prayer, founded by Graham Power, and the Lausanne Cape Town Congress in 2010."

Keith summarized his philanthropic decision making by saying that continuous prayer is important to guide decisions. If one feels in touch with the Lord, then the philanthropy will feel aligned. It is also important to give proportionally to one's financial capacity.

He also commented on the importance of understanding setbacks. "Many of the positives in my philanthropy have only happened after a series of ups and downs, challenges, and set-backs. In my understanding and learning from these past three to four decades, these helped me to strengthen my faith, stay humble, and remain prayerfully dependent on the Lord. In my experience, God wants to know whether we are truly committed and obedient regardless of the outcome."[2]

Isaiah and the Poor

Caring for the poor is one of the major threads of Isaiah. He saw God as providing refuge for the poor and shade from the heat. God invites us with our philanthropy to provide ways for the poor to thrive and to find solace in God.

POINTS TO CONSIDER

1. God has been faithful generationally to us, using divine circumstances.
2. Parents and grandparents play an important role in shaping our values of stewardship.
3. God wants to see how committed we are to a project regardless of the results.

A PRAYER

Jesus, thank you for your generosity and dogged faithfulness to us over the years. You are our shade and refuge. We cling to you as the Great Intercessor. Amen.

9

Nations

PASTOR JUNG-HYUN OH, SAM KO, AND SUNKI BANG UNITED TO REACH KOREA AND THE WORLD

> See, darkness covers the earth and thick darkness is over the peoples, but the LORD rises upon you and his glory appears over you.
>
> Isaiah 60:1–2

Isaiah saw a day when people and countries living in great darkness would experience the glory of the Lord. He would be stunned to see what has happened across Asia in the past one hundred years. Asia today has the greatest number of first-generation Christians and the largest missionary force per capita in Korea.

No greater spiritual contrast exists in the world today than between Christian South Korea and atheistic North Korea. Outside of SaRang Church in Korea is a Christmas tree with 2,300 red ornament balls. Each ball represents a church in North Korea that has disappeared under communism.

The modern Korean missions movement is one of the great mission movements of the past two thousand years. The early missionary Jermaine Robert Thomas came to Korea from Wales in 1866. He was beheaded that same year. Horace Underwood came from the United States in 1885. These pioneer missionaries helped plant Christianity in Korea.

As Doug Birdsall was preparing for the Lausanne Cape Town Congress in 2010, he met with Korean leaders to involve them in shaping the Congress. They invited Kyeong-Ju, a young North Korean woman who shared this story:

> I am from Pyongyang, the capital of North Korea. I am eighteen years old and the only child of my parents. Our relatives shared the gospel with us and we became Christian in 1992. For six years, my family experienced political persecution. We fled to China in 1998. My mother was pregnant with her second child but died from leukemia before she could give birth.
>
> Even during this suffering my father started a Bible study. In 2001 he was arrested by the Chinese police. He was in prison for three years. After he was released he chose to go back to North Korea.
>
> In 2006 he was discovered by the North Korean government and imprisoned. I have not had any contact with my father for four years. I believe that he was probably shot to death for treason in public by the North Korean government.[1]

Doug received generous support of $1.7 million from Korean pastors and business leaders for the 2010 Cape Town Congress. One of those leaders was Pastor Sam Ko, who was instrumental in securing financial support for the Congress in collaboration with Doug.

SaRang Global Ministries

Sam leads SaRang Global Ministries for the SaRang Church in Seoul. When I interviewed him, he mentioned he had been senior pastor for a season at Korean Church of Queens, near my home, from 2005 to 2007. We knew several of the same families that have been part of KCQ.

As we spoke, Sam described his sense of identity as Korean by race, American by place, Canadian by choice, and Christian by grace. He traveled extensively to study in the United States, led churches in the United States, ran a business in Canada, and returned to Korea to lead the SaRang Church's mission effort. SaRang Church has grown from a founding group of nine people to thirty-five thousand members today. After seeing God's hand on their church, the leadership felt the need to give back to the world. Sam stepped into his role as leader of Global Ministries, after being invited by senior pastor Jung-Hyun Oh to do so. Pastor Jung-Hyun Oh has led SaRang Church into an extraordinary season of discipleship training and missions engagement.

As SaRang Church looked at the world, they saw a particularly significant need in Europe. After an exchange of many emails with Wales Evangelical School of Theology (WEST), a partnership was formed with Sam serving as the board chair. The vision was to train young men and women to become leaders in a spiritually arid part of Western Europe. Coming to Wales was expressing gratitude for the early witness of Jermaine Robert Thomas in 1866.

Over a six-year period WEST's new campus building has been stabilized to serve 130 Welsh and British Christian students. Many churches across Wales had been closed, and this was the first time in a long time a new church building had been built.

At the close of their thanksgiving service, a Welsh man stepped forward with an envelope containing £430,000. The gift was enough to pay for surrounding property.

Then, a new vision was born in 2013 to plant a new church in each of the twelve surrounding valleys in Wales, and it is expanding to plant one thousand churches across Europe.

The short-term goal was to plant fifty new churches by June 2017. Projects are starting in Ukraine, Serbia, Romania, Albania, Macedonia, Finland, Italy, the United Kingdom, and in Macedonia. In Macedonia the project is called "The New Macedonian Vison Project," a project to plant and to revitalize one hundred churches by 2019.

E-land

Doug Birdsall also introduced me to Sunki Bang, who lives in Seoul. He has served as chaplain to the E-land Company for the past twenty-six years. E-land is one of the largest corporations in Korea, working in the fashion industry. Sunki told me he had also lived in Flushing, near my home.

The connection with Sunki was made as the company made a $1 million gift to the Lausanne Congress. The owner of the company is elder Song Soo Park.

Sunki and Park were students together and became good friends. Together they have enlisted sixty chaplains to serve the company. The vision is to use this as a training opportunity for younger leaders. Sunki says, "We have had several hundred employees participate in worship services throughout the company." The E-land company supports missions programs, including Korean missionaries around the world. It also supports international causes.

I asked Sam and Sunki what principles of leadership and philanthropy are important to them. Sam responded, "Korean pastors have great zeal and passion. We are lacking in opportunities to work with other global leaders. In order to make an impact on Europe, we have to work behind the scenes. We need to be like John the Baptist, saying Jesus must increase as I decrease."[2]

Sunki said, "It is very important that Christian business leaders learn how to share the gospel in the context of the marketplace. These same leaders must also manage their businesses as Christian leaders in all areas of ethics."[3]

Isaiah and Witnessing

Isaiah saw a time when God's people would be a witness to the world. The story of Korean Christianity and Korean missions is a story of the gospel coming to a nation and going to the nations.

POINTS TO CONSIDER

1. God has used the diaspora experiences of Korean Christians to reach the world through global missions.
2. The generosity of Korean Christians has created an enormous accelerant for the gospel.
3. Korean Christianity was planted with great sacrifice by early pioneers, and it will require great sacrifice to plant Christianity in the hard places of the globe, like Europe.

A PRAYER

Jesus, thank you for the martyrs who planted Christianity in Korea. Thank you for the Korean church, which shares the gospel radically around the world. Increase our sense of radical commitment to the gospel. Amen.

10

Harvest

PETER AND GAIL OCHS'S
MULTIGENERATIONAL VISION

You have enlarged the nation and increased their joy;
they rejoice before you as people rejoice at the harvest.

Isaiah 9:3

Isaiah was a national prophet for Israel, yet his writings consistently reflected God's inclusive kingdom. Isaiah 7 and 9 feature the messianic promise that a Savior was coming who would create a harvest embracing the entire world. When this harvest comes, the Bibles says, there will be extraordinary joy as the gospel goes forth and invites the nations into the family of God. Isaiah gives us a sense of a future fulfillment.

I was introduced to Peter Ochs by Doug Birdsall, executive director of Lausanne and the Cape Town 2010 Congress. Doug described Peter and Gail as his "favorite ministry investors." He said he discovered from Peter and Gail that the transformation that takes place between an investor and a ministry project is the "exchange of one joy for another joy."[1]

Peter and Gail have been married for fifty-one years and have four daughters and eleven grandchildren. They grew up on the same street in Bethlehem, Pennsylvania, and began dating at the end of high school. Peter began his own personal philanthropy at the age of thirteen when he began to tithe.

They have described their philanthropic journey as a partnership. They have observed that women are outliving men, so it is critically important that wives are fully involved in making philanthropic decisions with their husbands.

The Ochs are two of the most highly respected voices in Christian philanthropy in the United States. They have given philanthropic leadership through the Fieldstone and First Fruit foundations for the past few decades. Ochs made his personal wealth in the California real-estate market. "He commanded the respect of all his peers in the industry," said Sanford Goodkin, a real estate consultant in San Diego. "Ochs was a businessman who happened to be a home builder—but he could have headed any Fortune 500 company. He was elegant, disciplined, and an excellent leader."[2]

Ochs's start as a builder came early. A *Los Angeles Times* article said, "At 9 years old Peter Ochs could be found on his father's construction sites collecting stray nails in a tin can—the sixth generation of his family to show a passion for building. The nails eventually formed a kingdom of homes, as Ochs grew to create the largest privately owned home builder in Southern California."[3]

First Fruit

The First Fruit foundation website describes the significance of its work:

History

Guided by a Christian faith that integrates both word and deed, Peter and Gail decided to create a family foundation in

1976. They called the foundation First Fruit, a biblical reference which speaks to giving the best of our harvest as an offering to the Lord. The earliest years were spent giving grants to individuals the Ochs knew who were working in far-flung parts of the developing world. From the outset, they identified as globalists rather than tied to one region.

The Early Years

By the 1980s Dr. David Bennett arrived to help the organization sharpen its focus and begin to build a long-term strategy, eventually also joining the board.

In 1990 Rob Martin became the foundation's first executive director. First Fruit now had someone actively on the ground, seeking grants and working with ministries around the world.

From 1999 to 2001, Dr. Bennett developed the seminal *India Leadership Study*, which led to the unleashing of considerable resources by myriad donors to previously unknown ministries in India.

Our Growth

By the early 2000s the foundation was expanding the scale of its grant making rapidly and the Ochs family's next generation was beginning to get involved in both board and staff roles.

In 2005 Paul Park was hired to succeed Mr. Martin, allowing the latter to shift his focus on coaching and mentoring ministry leaders to develop their capacities and flourish in their callings. While celebrating the impact of more than two thousand grants in over one hundred countries, the foundation began a period of both self-reflection and experimentation, recognizing the world was changing rapidly.

Our Passion

In accordance with the Ochs's original intent, the foundation will sunset over the coming decades. From its first grant to its last, First Fruit will remain committed to supporting Christian organizations operating in the developing world, always valuing relationships, continuously asking for the wisdom of God, and seeking his perfect will.[4]

> To give away money is an easy matter and in any man's power. But to decide to whom to give it, how large and when, and for what purpose and how, is neither in every man's power nor an easy matter. Hence, it is that such excellence is rare, praiseworthy, and noble.[5]
>
> Aristotle

The Ochs and I shared about our common passion for India and the opportunity they would have to visit Bihar, India, for the first time in 2017. Since Marya and I made our first visit there in 1983, we have seen some of the transformative work that has taken place in that corner of the world in all its vast need. Regions like Bihar have indeed seen a gospel harvest because of the generosity and strategic engagement of the Ochs.[6]

Isaiah and the Harvest

Isaiah saw the day when people from every tribe and tongue would be a part of a gospel harvest. Couples like the Ochs are carrying out a multigenerational vision strategically and intelligently making an impact on regions of the world that have had limited access to the gospel.

POINTS TO CONSIDER

1. God can use the professional success of Jesus followers to gain an audience for the gospel.

2. It is important to surround one's self with colleagues who have done the important research and can provide the most effective vehicles to give strategically.

3. Identifying indigenous leaders in hard places like India is strategic to advance the gospel among unreached people groups.

4. Giving as a couple is an important spiritual discipline and is a great model for young Christian couples.

A PRAYER

Jesus, you are the Great Harvester. May you multiply the generosity of your people into the next generation to meet the needs of a world exploding in need. Amen.

11

Word

HOW GOD OPENED DOORS FOR DG AND GINI ELMORE

The grass withers and the flowers fall, but the word of our God endures forever.

Isaiah 40:8

In chapter 40 Isaiah contrasted the temporary nature of earthly kings and the eternality of God, especially in his Word. For thirty-nine chapters, Isaiah had been writing about the rise and fall of kingdoms in Israel and all its surrounding nations. Isaiah 40 is a pivotal chapter in the book. It points us toward John the Baptist, who would announce the imminent arrival of God's eternal Son.

Navigators is an organization raised up after World War II to emphasize the centrality of Scripture in the life of a disciple. They have had an extraordinarily fruitful ministry among the military, on college campuses, and now in cities. The organization is led by board chair DG Elmore.

I met DG in 2011 as the result of a wedding in Dallas he attended with Jim Runyan, our New York City Leadership Center board chair. DG's interest was sufficiently piqued in our work in New York City to prompt an introduction. We began to explore a partnership in the NYCMP that Bob Doll, Tim Keller, and I had helped to launch.

I was having dinner in a Dallas restaurant in December when Bob suddenly appeared on its television, giving a market report. At that same instant, a text from DG arrived, indicating he was committed to the project. It was a surreal moment.

Beginnings

DG grew up in a Chicago suburb. He describes some of his early spiritual influences. "My parents sent my siblings and me to a local church. I attended church until the fourth grade. In high school in my freshman year I attended the Fellowship of Christian Athletes. I attended on a weekly basis. In my junior year, my diving coach explained to me how Jesus was the fulfillment of hundreds of years of prophecy. I remember committing my life to Christ on a Wednesday night in February 1975."

In our interview, DG commented that he did not rigorously follow up on that commitment in high school. But when he attended Southern Methodist University for college, he began to participate in a Bible study, and he experienced huge spiritual growth as a member of Phi Gamma Delta. A student at Dallas Theological Seminary was also an important influence.

DG decided to take a joint MBA/Law degree program at Indiana University in Bloomington from 1980 to 1984, where he was introduced to Navigators. He got involved with a Bible study and was profoundly molded by Navigator staff. He states, "My experience with Navigators at Indiana University was transformative. It has shaped the direction of my spiritual life for the past thirty years."

DG and his wife, Gini, began dating in high school. When they went to different colleges they wrote letters to each other every day—more than twelve hundred of them. Gini made a faith commitment in 1977. DG and Gini have modeled a forty-year spiritual journey as a couple.

Family and Professional Journey

The Elmores have six children from their early twenties to mid-thirties. I have met one of the daughters, Lauren, who is now running one of the Elmore companies. We had DG and Lauren present on a panel at Movement Day 2015 in New York City on the theme of legacy. DG commented, "It has always been a high priority to invest in each of our six children. One of the ways we have celebrated our family life together is allowing each of the six children to choose a vacation spot that we will all travel to."

DG describes his professional journey. "God continues to open doors, and I have walked through them. My father had a travel agency, and I was a part of helping to turn that agency around in 1989. Over the past twenty-five years, I began to acquire companies. I began to ask myself, 'What is possible?'"

In 1993 DG owned three companies. He wrestled with the question, Is it healthy and acceptable to God to pursue growth and leverage businesses into something bigger? Between 1995 and 2005 he bought two companies per year. The net worth of those companies (minor league baseball teams) grew from

$15 million in revenue in 1995 to $100 million in revenue in 2015.

Philanthropic Journey

The Elmores have been involved in a diversity of causes. Gini serves on the board of the Bowery Mission in New York City, the third-oldest rescue mission in the United States. DG describes why he and Gini have been involved with the Bowery. "Ed Morgan, the CEO of the Bowery, helped us to understand the Bible has two thousand verses regarding the poor."

Beyond their philanthropy with Navigators, DG has a deep commitment to be a proactive board chair with the Navigators. He makes it a point to meet with each board member twice throughout the year, one-on-one.

DG remembers the first large financial pledge he made, in 1990. It was a $15,000 commitment over three years to a Navigators project. God made it possible for him to fulfill that pledge. He commented, "I saw the benefit of large pledges. Giving is a drain plug on greed."

I asked DG why he had become so deeply involved with the NYC Movement Project. He responded, "Cities empower all walks of life. I see the influence of New York City. If the gospel accelerates here, it will impact the whole world. We need to keep laboring together in the harvest field of global cities."

DG sees Movement Day (a critical leg in the NYC Movement Project) as a catalyst for people coming together to encourage each other and to learn. DG, Bob Doll, and Raymond Harris have worked closely together as the most prominent voices in the marketplace leader forums attached to Movement Day. Their bond of friendship has been a tremendous model for other marketplace leaders around the world. DG says, "This is about stewardship. Movement Day generates thinking for people who want to deeply impact their cities."[1]

Isaiah and the Word

Isaiah reminds us that the Scriptures are eternal and transcend the momentary political and economic realities. They give us the perspective to live all of life. In Isaiah 40 the prophet gives us God's perspective on his own Word—that it will never pass away.

POINTS TO CONSIDER

1. The speed of spiritual growth is in proportion to the depth of commitment to study the Scriptures.
2. God uses the generosity of his people as a safeguard against greed in our lives.
3. Spending time with family members, colleagues, and board members in deepening, intimate relationships is important to advance the kingdom of God.

A PRAYER

Jesus, you are the Word of God made flesh. Inhabit our hearts and inhabit your world afresh as we obey you with all our hearts. Speak into the affairs of cities and the circumstances of the poor through your Word this day. Amen.

12

Friendship

WHEN RAYMOND AND MARYDEL HARRIS FELT THE CALL TO MINISTRY THROUGH BUSINESS

> But you, Israel, my servant, Jacob, whom I have chosen, you descendants of Abraham my friend, I took you from the ends of the earth, from its farthest corners I called you. I said, "You are my servant."
>
> Isaiah 41:8–9

Isaiah introduces us to one of the great mysteries of the Bible. God is our Cosmic King, yet he invites us to enter friendship with him. Abraham was described as a friend of God. Jesus told his disciples the night before he was crucified that he no longer called them servants, but friends.

One of the most remarkable friendship journeys I have experienced has been with Raymond and Marydel Harris. Over the past five years, I have enjoyed the hospitality of their home dozens of times. Through our mutual relationships, we have seen that friendship begets more friendships, and friendships in the gospel can bear extraordinary fruit and change history.

I met Raymond for the first time at a Movement Day breakfast in 2011 at Park Cities Baptist Church in Dallas. We were introduced by Mario Zandstra, CEO of Pine Cove Christian Camps at the time. Raymond and his wife, Marydel, came to visit New York City to hear Tim Keller speak in January 2012. Friendship begets friendship.

We quickly developed our friendship as the Harrises hosted me in their home. I was immediately struck by the breadth of their relationships around the world. They have engaged with dozens of leaders and agencies over their nearly forty years of marriage.

The couple met at the University of Oklahoma in the 1970s. Raymond earned his master's degree in architecture and Marydel earned a degree in education. They were active with Campus Crusade for Christ and married at the end of their senior year.

At the end of their university years, the Harrises were invited on the staff of Campus Crusade. They made the difficult decision to instead launch into an architectural career and raise a family. They moved to Dallas, where Raymond began an architectural firm. He was in his midtwenties.

Landing the Walmart Account

As a start-up architectural firm, Raymond's business, RHA Associates, was committed to the principle of excellence in small things to create larger opportunities. Raymond wrote in his book *The Anatomy of a Successful Firm*:

> When I set out to establish my new firm, I began to ponder what makes other firms successful. What appealed to me in 1983 were

the well-established, medium-to-large firms with solid reputa-
tions. That was my goal: to be well established, reputable, and
known for integrity. I observed that these firms were usually
established by outstanding practitioners who started small with
a strong work ethic and developed a clientele over time.[1]

When Raymond was twenty-seven, his firm landed an account with Walmart. Raymond describes the parallel growth
of their firm alongside Walmart's growth. "We diligently served
Walmart by providing these remodeling services for several
years, resulting in thousands of projects over the next twenty-
five years. Every remodel designed since 1993 has been done
using master specifications prepared and maintained by RHA."

Repeatable excellence in his craft provided tremendous professional opportunities. By the firm's 25th anniversary, RHA
Associates had employed 213 staff, with many of their team
minority architects. The firm became the number-two design
firm in the United States for retail architecture, according to
McGraw-Hill's *Architectural Record*.[2]

The Harrises have viewed the success of the company from
a spiritual plane. Raymond writes in his book *The Heart of
Business*, "If there is one thing I am sure of, God has richly
blessed our business. Over the past thirty years He has provided
a significant amount of profitable work throughout the United
States, and I can find no other explanation than He chose to
bless our firm for his own purposes. We don't deserve it, and
the recession of recent years argues against any natural cause.
We are clearly recipients of His sovereign goodness."[3]

Friends to Younger and Global Leaders

The Harrises have been deeply involved in discipling young
couples in the theme of stewardship. For many years in their

living room they have taught small groups about the principles of living debt free. Along with Chuck Bentley from Crown Ministries, they helped to found The Christian Economic Forum. Raymond has traveled globally with Crown Ministries to Africa, South America, and Asia, teaching on stewardship.

The Harrises have also been involved in assisting younger leaders through mentorship relationships. A particular interest to them has been helping young filmmakers create and market their films. Jon and Andrew Erwin have directed a series of remarkable films titled *October Baby*, *Moms' Night Out*, and *Woodlawn*. The Harrises explain their interest in helping them to be successful in the film industry. "We believe that film is an important vehicle to speak into the values of our culture about spiritual truth."

The couple also embodied this discipleship ethic at home as Raymond journeyed with his two sons through Boy Scouts and as Marydel engaged with her daughters in their school projects. Marydel also served as PTA president four times during her children's school years. And she has had a remarkable ministry to women in her community Bible study, administrating a group of seventy who gather together.

The Harrises have always been drawn to care for the poor globally and domestically. In recent years they have been involved with International Justice Mission. Their spiritual values are deeply aligned with God's concern for the oppressed. They have often said, "God's heart is for the poor. We can become spiritually rich by lending to the poor."

Raymond and Marydel have also been involved in an entrepreneurial effort with John Enright, through Bee Sweet. John has given extraordinary leadership to empower African farmers to become economically independent. Raymond says, "You've got to understand, what we're doing is nuts. We've made fifty thousand beehives and we're giving them all away—this is insane."

Bee Sweet, headquartered in Ndola, Zambia, has spent the last eight years perfecting its business model. The company currently contracts about twelve thousand rural households, which oversee seventy thousand hives. According to Raymond, in 2014 Bee Sweet harvested 150 tons of its light amber, polyfloral honey and paid out about $100,000 to smallholder farmers across Zambia's Miombo forests.

Domestically, Marydel has served as a board member to Elevate USA, which works to transform cities by building long-term, life-changing relationships with urban youth. Elevate USA is in multiple cities across the United States.

The Call to Friendship: Movement Day

Early in our relationship, the Harrises extended a great sign of their friendship to me—they gave me a key to their front door. Marya and I also have visited their home in Jackson Hole on multiple occasions. Raymond and I have traveled together to France and the United Kingdom. He sums it up best when he says, "The gospel goes forward at the speed of friendship."

The Harrises, along with the Dolls (Bob and Leslie) and the Elmores (DG and Gini), anchored the initial efforts related to the NYC Movement Project and Movement Day. Along with others, these three couples have leveraged their generosity, their credibility, and their friendship to bring a dream to reality—to measurably reach New York City with the gospel and to catalyze expressions of the gospel globally through New York City. The fruit of the project over five years was seen in sixty NYC churches planted, twenty-six thousand leaders trained, and fourteen thousand leaders from four hundred cities attending Movement Day.

It has been such a powerful discipleship principle—that to go far with a vision you become close to a few friends around a big idea. The Harrises have an extraordinary gift of hospitality. They have modeled excellence in so many areas of their lives—in the home, with their stewardship, and professionally. Raymond summarized his and Marydel's stewardship callings as taking place in the following dimensions:

- Journeying with ministry colleagues (like Movement Day)
- Creating for profit enterprises to empower the poor
- Investing in millennial leaders
- Providing thought leadership content by writing books on stewardship themes[4]

Isaiah and Friendship

Isaiah could be disruptive in his generation because he had a friendship with God. As a prophet, he had the clearest understanding of the coming of the Messiah of any writer in the Old Testament. God could trust Isaiah with his revelation because Isaiah responded with radical obedience as a friend to God.

POINTS TO CONSIDER

1. A commitment to excellence in the beginning creates future opportunities.
2. Investing in young and entrepreneurial leaders creates long-term impact.
3. The gospel spreads at the speed of friendship.

A PRAYER

Jesus, we thank you that you are the friend of sinners. You disrupted the world by creating a community of friends who laid down their lives for one another. Amen.

13

Joy

SCOTT AND HOLLY WITTMAN PARTNER WITH HABITAT FOR HUMANITY

You will go out in joy and be led forth in peace; the
mountains and hills will burst into song before you.

Isaiah 55:12

Isaiah's final chapters burst forth with a joy that permeates all
of creation and the multitudes experiencing God's salvation.
God is at work redeeming creation, which has been groan-
ing since the cosmic splinter that took place in Genesis 3. At
the end of Revelation, all of creation is restored. Wrongs are
righted. The poor are cared for and the orphan is enveloped
into God's family. God is providentially at work to bring this
to pass.

I met Pastor Bret Nicholson at Willow Creek Community
Church in 2012. That meeting led to a visit to Evansville, Indi-

ana, in December, and there I met Scott's brother, who recommended that Scott and I meet.

That introduction led to a phone call with Scott in February 2013. He was now living in California, working with American Century Investments. We agreed that I would visit him later that year. We met twice in the coming months, and I was sitting in a movie theater over Christmas holiday that same year when I learned Scott agreed to join our team as an investor in the New York City Movement Project. He sent me an email confirming that commitment.

Indiana Roots

Scott grew up in rural Indiana. He describes the early years. "I gained a sense of the wonder of God's creation and living off the land. It was in that context that I developed an early faith in the Lutheran heritage of my family."

Scott's paternal family had emigrated from Germany. His dad worked for the Department of Agriculture and his mom worked in the school cafeteria.

He describes the early impact of his family on his faith. "We were deeply grounded in our faith with a strong reliance on Scripture. We believed in the creeds by faith alone and by Scripture alone. I saw the importance of living in the world and relying on Scripture as well as the benefit of believers being brought together." Scott has retained his roots in the Missouri Synod Lutheran Church. He currently serves as the board chair of Concordia College in Westchester County north of New York City, a Missouri Synod school.

Scott met his wife, Holly, in college, where they both earned undergraduate and master's degrees. Scott earned degrees in finance and an MBA. After college he held positions in Pittsburgh and Los Angeles. Then the family moved to New York.

New York City and Back to the Midwest

Scott became the president of Vantage Global Advisors and served in that role for six years. During that tenure, he began attending a Harvard Club breakfast group in midtown Manhattan. The purpose of the breakfast was to create an environment where Christian marketplace leaders could hear a relevant message for their calling in the marketplace.

During the Harvard Club meetings, Scott was introduced to the teaching of Tim Keller, who spoke there every month. The years of working in Manhattan were formative. When we spoke, Scott commented, "Holly and I determined that it was great news for my career to have so much responsibility at such a young age. We also determined that it was bad news to have so much responsibility at such a young age with a young family."

After nine years in New York City, Scott decided to leave the business world to spend time with extended family, all of whom were in the Midwest. He and Holly relocated to Indiana. Scott says, "I had done some volunteering for Habitat for Humanity. I was interested in doing more, and I contacted them. I began to volunteer as a treasurer for a local affiliate. I then joined the executive committee."

Then a difficulty emerged. Habitat was planning a "blitz build" in less than six months—twenty-five houses in one week—and the executive director resigned six months before the build. Scott says, "As the treasurer, I asked at the next meeting, 'Where can we find an executive director to take over the leadership with the build in six months?' My wife, Holly, told me, 'You can do that!'"

Scott stepped into that role for the next three years. Describing the wonder of the blitz build, he says, "We involved two thousand volunteers. We built twenty-five homes in one section of Evansville that was completely transformed. I could see families when they applied for housing and then see them as they achieved the dream of home ownership. The volunteers were living out their faith. It was an absolutely remarkable experience."

Scott currently serves American Century Investments as the chief investment officer for asset allocation and disciplined equity. He describes his vocational calling. "All jobs are about serving other people. We serve people's financial needs focused on retirement savings. We help people realize their retirement goals and objectives."

Being a Strategic Investor

I asked Scott why he got involved in the NYC Movement Project as an investor. He said, "I see how incredibly strategic New York City is for the church. I really got a strong sense of calling for the nine years I lived and worked in New York City. Tim Keller speaks about New York City as the financial and media capital of the world. I have been so deeply encouraged to see the church of New York City thriving over the past twenty years. This has been incredibly powerful and necessary to stimulate the church in New York City to impact the world."

He also commented, "My first job growing up was cutting grass. I earned five dollars a week. My dad taught me how to handle this money by giving the first 10 percent to the church. I say to people it is all about developing a habit of doing the right things over a long period. I believe that we are called through the parable of the talents to steward everything we have—our time, our talent, and our treasure."[1]

Isaiah and the Theme of Joy

Isaiah wrote in chapter 55 of the miracle of coming to God with our thirst and hunger without money, yet he will provide for us. God can do the supernatural with what we have or what we don't have to meet a larger purpose. When he meets that purpose, the result is joy.

POINTS TO CONSIDER

1. Generational faithfulness results in present impact.
2. Our marketplace calling is an expression of service to others.
3. Making an impact on cities like New York will make an impact on the world.

A PRAYER

Jesus, you are the Great Multiplier. Help us to respond to you in joy when we see you at work using the simple offerings we bring to you. You are extraordinarily active all around us. Amen.

14

Rebuild

PHIL AND MELISSA SHAFFER MEET NEEDS IN COLUMBUS, OHIO

> They will rebuild the ancient ruins and restore the
> places long devastated.
>
> Isaiah 61:4

Isaiah 61 is the passage Jesus chose as his "inaugural address" in Luke 4 to describe his mission. He quoted the passage about giving sight to the blind and preaching good news to the poor. Jesus's mission, as prophesied by Isaiah, was to rebuild lives, cities, and cultures. Nowhere is this passage more applicable than in urban America and the great cities of the globe.

In March 2013 I received a text message from a close friend, Doug Slaybaugh, introducing me to Phil Shaffer. Phil was arriving that day from Columbus, Ohio. I remember him hustling down a Manhattan street to make sure we could connect. He was an absolute sponge in learning about what God had done in New York City over the past thirty years. He had a similar passion for Columbus. Subsequent conversations resulted in Kevin Palau of the Luis Palau Association and me copresenting to a community of leaders in Columbus a year later. We cast vision for ways God was rebuilding urban America through churches working together.

The gospel movement in Columbus was ready to rapidly accelerate to a new level, and rarely have I met a successful marketplace leader with a hunger to learn, invest, and implement strategic efforts as enormous as Phil Shaffer's.

Early Days

During our interview, Phil described his early days in Columbus. "I was the fourth of four boys. My parents divorced when I was seven years old. That divorce was profoundly impactful. My mom raised me until I went away to college. She began to engage her faith after the divorce."

Phil was witnessed to at the College of Wooster, a liberal arts college where he studied business and history. While still in college he interned at Head Start Columbus. This experience planted seeds in his life to make an impact for the marginalized of the city.

After college, when Phil was looking for work, he cried out to God, "If you're real, lead me to a place to have a career. Lead me to people who know you so I can know you." He landed a job in Dayton, and he was overwhelmed by the reception of his boss and coworkers. He told them, "You guys love me more than anyone who has loved me. What is going on?" Phil's colleagues had a deep faith commitment. Two months later he became a Christian. Immediately he began to learn about and practice tithing.

Phil's wife, Melissa, grew up in a large family in Dayton, the sixth of seven children. Her dad worked nights in a tire factory. The family always practiced generosity, for instance, by giving to others from their acre garden. Her mother was active in her Christian faith.

Phil and Melissa eventually met at a church in Dayton. Before they began dating, they were both inspired by the church's funding campaign. Phil says, "As a young Christian, I felt challenged to give $50,000 above my tithe over a three-year period. I was looking for confirmation when the pastor communicated that he believed God was leading someone to make a pledge of that size." He began to weep. "I learned that I had the gift of giving, and that was one of the ways that God showed me who he was."

At the time, Melissa was only sixteen years old and worked after school and in summer jobs. Still, she felt challenged to give $2,000 above her tithe.

A Passion for Career and Columbus

In 1979 Phil began working in the financial services industry with EF Hutton, then with Smith Barney, and eventually with Morgan Stanley from 2008 onward. During his demanding career, he began the journey of self-discovery. He took a course called Prime Movers, created by a high school friend, Chip Ingram.

When I interviewed the couple, Phil commented, "I discovered my holy ambition in Prime Movers. I realized that I needed to drive change and action. I wanted to see a disruption in the status quo." Melissa also participated in Prime Movers. She said, "I have a passion for people to find wholeness and healing. I have a background in counseling, and I really long for people to discover wholeness."

Phil saw a natural connection to the vison of a city gospel movement with his holy ambition, and he was inspired by Tim Keller and his writings. His interest in New York City coincided with his son, daughter-in-law, and grandchild living there.

In 2014 and 2015, Phil was helping Columbus colleagues Krista Sisterhen and Scott Mallory apply some of the lessons learned in New York City, and I was privileged to travel to Columbus several times to cast vision for establishing a citywide prayer expression.

In 2014 and 2015, citywide Columbus concerts of prayer were held in African American churches for nearly one thousand people each year. In 2016 the citywide prayer gathering attracted thirty-five hundred people from eighty churches. A forty days of prayer effort called Pray for Columbus was established. Phil commented, "Megachurch pastors were coming together in Columbus in a way that had never happened before. They were weeping out of joy in being together and seeing the walls come down in our city."

Plans are under way to grow several church-school partnerships across Columbus. The city is fortunate to have several mature, long-term efforts making an impact on young people, planting churches, and engaging the marketplace.

Phil told me, "In the fall of 2016 you could feel and taste the impact of all of this in Columbus. Already 15 percent of the schools have been adopted. Kevin Palau and you have coached us on the priority of being rooted in prayer and the unity of the body. It exists in Columbus and it is supernatural. It can only come out of prayer. We are seeing marketplace leaders engaged to help us figure out how to do job creation. We need to be interrupted by God's plans for our city."

Phil has been an important adviser to the global expansion of Movement Day. He joined us in London in December 2015. He says, "I envision so many of the great principles and models established in New York City being replicated by cities all over the world."[1]

Isaiah and the Rebuilding of Cities

Isaiah saw the engagement of the faith community as the difference maker in the context of cities. He saw a day when cities would recover from a season of abandonment and neglect. When God's people come together to seek the health and prosperity of their cities, an entire generation of young people improves their lives.

POINTS TO CONSIDER

1. God honors radical generosity and increases people's spiritual influence through their giving.
2. Taking the posture of learner is the place to start when fostering a city gospel movement.
3. Prayer is the place to start building trust across racial and denominational divides.

A PRAYER

Jesus, you see cities like Columbus, which need to be rebuilt. Open our eyes to the communities of need in our own cities. Help us find others with a similar passion to rebuild. Amen.

15

Fruitful

LEW BAKES AND TONY LEMBKE FIND A COMMON CALLING TO SERVE LEADERS

In a very short time, will not Lebanon be turned into a fertile field and the fertile field seem like a forest?

Isaiah 29:17

Isaiah saw a day when Israel, despite their uneven obedience, would experience tremendous fruitfulness. Throughout the book of Isaiah, he pointed to a day when God would include nations once far off—he had surprises in store as the Great Includer among the nations. Jesus pointed to our fruitfulness as a sign of our discipleship and authentic relationship with him.

Lew Bakes and Tony Lembke have been friends with a great legacy of fruitfulness toward ministry leaders in New York City.

Lewis Bakes

I met Lew Bakes after hosting the Global Leadership Summit in 2005 in Metro New York City. I was impressed with the passion of his faith and his willingness to jump in with both feet to advance the gospel. Over the next three years, Lew was instrumental, along with a small core group of area marketplace Christians, in launching the New York City Leadership Center. We had dozens of meetings in his home in New Canaan, Connecticut.

Lew grew up in the northeastern part of the United States, in a Greek Orthodox household where the church was the cultural and religious hub of the family. His father, Charles, is a first-generation American who grew up during the Depression and worked in his family's business. Charles modeled hard work, discipline, and entrepreneurship.

Lew says of his mother, Portia, who came to the United States as a teenager, "I remember my mother's daily routine of visiting the Greek Orthodox church in Stamford to visit with our family priest, pray, and light a candle. She was extremely dedicated to the church and had a laser focus when it came to taking care of her husband, her children, her family, and those who were unable to advocate for themselves. My mother modeled faith, family, community, and generosity."

Lew married the love of his life, Sandra, in 1982 and graduated from law school in 1983 with a JD and an LLM in taxation in 1984. In 1990, after practicing law and acting as general counsel for a real-estate development company, he cofounded ITDS, a provider of billing and customer care software to the wireless telecommunications industry. After a Lehman Brothers led IPO in 1996, Lew initiated the acquisition of a competing business in 1998 that resulted in ITDS becoming the second-largest company of its kind in the world.

After being in existence for ten years, ITDS was blessed to employ one thousand men and women whose work resulted in many awards, including being recognized at number 64 by Forbes in its 200 Best Small Companies list. In 2000, Lew initiated the sale of ITDS to Amdocs Limited, creating the world's largest provider of billing and customer care software to the wireless industry.

Lew describes his experience encountering Christ. "The day after the sale of ITDS, I had an overwhelming sense of emptiness. At that moment in my life, I had an amazing wife and children, and had overseen a very successful exit for ITDS's employees and investors, yet I was unfulfilled.

Lew commented, "On a beautiful August morning in 2001, while throwing a football to my son Dean, I noticed that a religious service was being performed in my neighbors' backyard. It was the following week that I attended one of the earliest services of Grace Church, where I was transformed and ultimately accepted Christ as my Lord and Savior."

Within a few short weeks of his conversion, the World Trade Towers came down in the 9/11 attacks on the United States and his mother was diagnosed with a terminal brain tumor. "I am convinced," he says, "that if I hadn't found Christ at that time in my life, my reaction to both of those traumatic events would have been dramatically different."

In our interview, Lew talked about the influences in his life in the coming years. "Sandy and I got actively involved in Grace Community Church and Young Life and helped start several Bible studies in our community. I also attended the Willow Creek Global Leadership Summit for the first time in 2003 and experienced how excellence and leadership could be modeled by a church."

Our lives intersected after the 2005 Global Leadership Summit Lew attended. He became an adviser to us in the formation of the NYC Leadership Center, which had a passion to catalyze leaders to change their cities. We recognized that we needed a different leadership and funding model. Lew suggested we follow Christ's disciple model and find twelve investors who would each commit one hundred thousand dollars a year for three years to launch the NYCLC. He was the first one in. Lew's model inspired other leaders to join the team. Within our first year, we had raised nearly $1 million. Lew helped anchor the launch and made several important trips with me to Willow Creek and other locations. He was a founding board member for the NYCLC.

I asked Lew what his primary passions were. He said, "I am passionate about my faith, my wife, my children, fitness, sports cars, and helping position marketplace Christians and Christian ministries for success. I pray Ephesians 3:20 several times a day, believing that God, who by his mighty power at work within us, is able to do far more than we would ever dare to ask or even dream of, beyond our highest prayers, desires, or hopes."

Lew is convinced the most effective way to position Christian ministries for success is by harnessing the energy of trained and engaged marketplace leaders.[1]

Tony Lembke

Tony Lembke was another member of the initial core group that launched the NYC Leadership Center in 2008. He attends The Presbyterian Church at New Providence in New Jersey, led by Jeff Ebert. Jeff invited Tony to a luncheon we had at the Hilton Hotel at 53rd and 6th Avenue, and within a few weeks Tony followed up with me. He wanted to join the core group of investors to launch the NYCLC. Tony felt a strong call to get involved when he heard that a goal was to create a "tipping point" of Christian grace to the world's most influential city and to bring leadership resources to pastors and Christian leaders in the NYC metro area.

Tony grew up in Indiana in a strict German Lutheran household and then finished high school in Michigan and attended the University of Michigan. In the summers, he worked on a farm and observed that if anyone should have faith, it's farmers. He was surrounded by great spiritual role models in his family, including his grandfather, who was a pastor in the Lutheran Church. Despite these role models, Tony was skeptical of religion.

He studied chemical engineering, landed a job in New Jersey with Exxon, and met his wife, Diane, who is originally from Long Island. After working in the field for a few years, he concluded that engineering wasn't the place he wanted to land. He wanted faster feedback on his ideas, and the capital markets offered that by the minute.

After leaving Exxon, Tony found himself working on Wall Street in mortgage-backed securities. He parlayed his quantitative skills into a role at a Wall Street investment bank, Kidder Peabody, in their mortgage-backed securities research group. This would begin a thirty-year career in the mortgage-backed market—the biggest bond market in the world. Tony became an "All American" analyst and then an award-winning investor who launched an investment fund in 1999 with just over $10 million and grew it to nearly $3 billion over the next fifteen years.

His professional development coincided with his spiritual development. He says, "I came back to Christianity in the 1980s. I eventually joined the firm MKP Capital. Chip Perkins was a committed Christian and became a good friend. I had a great deal of respect for his spiritual leadership."

Tony has been a cornerstone in the development of the NYCLC's Leadership Fellows Program. Every year fifty to seventy-five nonprofit leaders attend a nine-month training course. At the end of the course, students graduate with a two-year business plan. Tony has been an important faculty for LFP. He has taught on finding the place of your leadership genius and has also provided one-on-one coaching for Fellows students.

I asked Tony why he was so committed to the Leadership Fellows Program. He said, "What resonated with me was the idea that providing leadership resources to pastors and nonprofit leaders was a great leverage point. In making these leaders more effective, they could scale their impact by ten times or even one hundred times."[2] The Leadership Fellows has trained more than three hundred leaders in its first seven years. The 2015–16 cohort was making an impact on three hundred thousand people on a regular basis.

Isaiah and Fruitfulness

Isaiah wrote during a time of great turbulence and devastation nationally. Yet God told him about a future reality when the people of God would indeed be fruitful. Their fruitfulness would make an impact on the whole earth.

POINTS TO CONSIDER

1. God uses the professional success of marketplace leaders to give them a strategic and globally influential platform.
2. It takes only a small group of highly committed leaders to launch a world-changing organization.
3. Our fruitfulness can be exponential when aligned with leaders of common vision and excellence in execution.

A PRAYER

Jesus, your vision is to see a fruitful church. You want your glory to cover the earth as the waters cover the sea. Give favor to leaders who are collaborating all over the world to see you do immeasurably more. Amen.

16

Faithfulness

THE BALMER FAMILY'S HEART
FOR MISSIONS AND MINISTRY

LORD, you are my God; I will exalt you and praise
your name, for in perfect faithfulness you have done
wonderful things, things planned long ago.

Isaiah 25:1

One of the important themes of Isaiah is the faithfulness of
God down through the centuries. Despite all the political, spiritual, and economic upheaval going on his world, Isaiah saw
the hand of God guiding history. God's plans are perfectly,
though mysteriously, choreographed, and Isaiah declared that
God was his God. I have seen that emphatic theme in the life
of the Balmer family.

I met the Balmer family in 2008 at the introduction of Tim
Boal, a founding board member of the New York City Leadership Center. Boal was the executive director of Go 2 Ministries, a
national church-planting expression of the Fellowship of Grace

Brethren Churches. When I met the Balmer family, I was struck by their extraordinary hospitality.

Ken Balmer is the patriarch of the family. He and his wife, Ruth, hosted me in their home on my first trip to see them. They can trace their ancestry back to 1732, their ancestors having arrived in the United States before American independence, and today they have a multigenerational story that has affected people all over the world.

Ken remembers his own growing-up years. "I grew up on a one-hundred-acre farm. We had twenty cows, five hundred chickens, ten acres of wheat, and thirty acres of corn." Ken was a member of the Brethren Church and applied for 1-W status during the Korean War as a conscientious objector. He worked at a state hospital during the war and met Ruth, who was a nurse in training. They were married in 1956.

Penn Valley Gas

Ken's father-in-law invited him to copurchase a propane gas company in 1957. The former owner called the company the "the Lord's Business." Ken says, "It is still the Lord's business today." Today they run a family propane company in Pennsylvania— Penn Valley Gas.

Ken and Ruth's family also started in 1957 with the arrival of their son Dan. Today Dan, his brothers Dale and Dwane, and Dan's son, Josh, are the second- and third-generation owners of the company. Ken remembers, "That first year we bought gas for six cents per gallon. We filled twenty-pound tanks for thirty cents per gallon. The first year of the company we sold 126,000 gallons of gas."

For the past six decades, the company has grown steadily. The Lord has provided trusted employees to support that growth, many of whom are friends and family who share their values and work unto the Lord. In the 1960s they bought a tractor trailer that allowed them to transport gas and create a whole-sale operation.

The retail operation grew from 126,000 gallons delivered the first year to its present 8 million gallons of gas delivered to residential customers. Their total annual sales including businesses, homes, industrial plants, farms, and other propane retailers is now over 20 million gallons.

Spiritual Roots

The Balmers come from a deeply spiritual family tradition. It is remarkable to see the depth and warmth of faith across three generations. Dan's wife, Chris, went home to be with the Lord in November 2016. Her memorial service was standing room only—a vibrant testament to the impact Chris and the entire Balmer family have made in their community. I invited Dan and Chris's son, Josh, on our board at the formation of the New York City Leadership Center. Today they all worship at Penn Valley Church in Telford, Pennsylvania, near Philadelphia.

Ken remembers meeting his in-laws for the first time. "I was invited to Ruth's home for supper, and the family had devotions. That was new to me. I could tell Ruth's family loved the Lord. For the past sixty years, family devotions have become a part of the Balmer family culture."

Giving

The Balmers's spiritual values have translated into their philanthropic involvements. Ken often quotes 2 Corinthians 9:7:

"God loves a cheerful giver" along with the phrase "You can't out-give the Lord." They partner with the Grace Brethren in water projects across the Central African Republic (CAR). Ken describes this effort. "To drill for clean water in the CAR, you have to go down 200 feet on average, but sometimes as much as 450 feet. Clean water is essential to having a healthy life, and allowing children to grow, go to school, and contribute to improving their community. We learned that access to clean water adds decades to a person's life. Clean water is especially life changing for children, since 20 percent die before age five due to water-related diseases."

Josh remembers a trip to Africa with his grandparents. "One particular day it was really hot outside, over 100 degrees in the shade. I will never forget my grandfather outside in the heat, building benches for the newly built orphan care center. He was committed to being part of the team while we were there."

The Balmers are also big believers in church planting, and they have funded such efforts in diverse contexts. Internationally they have supported church plants in South America, Canada, Europe, and Africa. Locally they have partnered with Urban Hope in Philadelphia. Urban Hope is a community church that focuses on reaching children and youth, provides training for urban ministries, and hosts a degree program for Grace College.

In addition to supporting large projects, the Balmers have supported dozens of missionaries around the world. They have always used their home to host the missionaries they support. The Balmers believe hospitality is a way for angels to be present unaware (Hebrews 13:2). As one of the many guests who have found rest in their welcoming home, I've come to love Ruth's meals and believe she is indeed one of the best pie makers in North America.

Dan says, "Dad and Mom's hearts for God's mission were clearly taught and lived out before our family, which has been a true testament to their desire to pass their life-encompassing faith to the next generation. Our prayer would be to see the Lord continue this through future generations of our family."

The New York City Movement Project and Movement Day Global Cities

The Balmers were one of the early investors in the NYC Movement Project. They attended the Partner Reception in Manhattan in 2009 when we unveiled the research on Manhattan Church Planting. Josh says, "We resonate with the words of Henry Blackaby: 'Watch to see where God is at work and join him in his work.' That is why we eagerly got involved with the New York City Leadership Center."

Dan comments, "We love to support efforts with a gospel orientation. We saw in the NYC Movement Project an important foundation of prayer, the gospel being preached, and inner city leaders being resourced."[1]

The Balmers also invested specifically in Movement Day Global Cities. They were particularly committed to assisting African leaders to attend the gathering. Dan says, "We recognized that it takes leadership to bring the body of Christ together on such a large scale. The world is changing so fast, there is an urgent need to bring evangelical leaders together to work together."

In addition to assisting African leaders, the Balmer grant also provided scholarships for 140 Philadelphia leaders to gather in New York City, which included former mayor Wilson Goode. The impact of Movement Day Global Cities is already being seen in the multiplication of leaders gathering in unity across a dozen cities globally.

Isaiah and the Faithfulness of God

Despite the difficult political circumstances Isaiah found himself in, he extolled the perfect faithfulness of God. God is the architect of his perfect plan across generations, nations, and millennia. His ultimate act of faithfulness is in the gospel, as Jesus comes to rescue the cities of the world and all who live in them.

POINTS TO CONSIDER

1. God can create surprising opportunities in the marketplace for people at an early age.
2. Generational faithfulness to excellence in work and generosity creates enormous impact.
3. The faithfulness of one family can make an impact on both local and global communities.

A PRAYER

Jesus, we thank you for your perfect faithfulness. You have been generous to each of us through your people in an infinite number of ways. We celebrate your generosity. Amen.

17

Vision

ZACH AND REGAN CARLILE RECEIVED A VISION FOR GENEROSITY

> The vision concerning Judah and Jerusalem that
> Isaiah son of Amoz saw during the reigns of Uz-
> ziah, Jotham, Ahaz and Hezekiah, kings of Judah.
>
> Isaiah 1:1

The vision Isaiah saw concerning Judah and Jerusalem begins
the longest prophetic book of the Old Testament. Everything
begins with vision, because our vision of God will define our
lives and our major life choices. Because of the vision Isaiah
saw, he could see the sweep of God's work from the judgment
of Israel to the judgment of the nations, to the coming of the
Messiah, and to the inclusion of the Gentiles in the grand cli-
max of salvation history.

Big visions inspire grand gestures. Zach and Regan Carlile
received a vision of God for their lives and family at an early

stage of their marriage. I met Zach through a mutual friend, Mario Zandstra, in Dallas (see chapter 12). Zach and Regan are also huge fans of the writings of Tim Keller, and they were inspired by his vision to reach New York City.

I found Zach to be one of the most thoughtful forty-year-olds I had ever met. He told me in our first meeting, "Keller's book *Counterfeit Gods* was revolutionary for me. As a businessman working in the energy industry, I realized how easy it is for money to become an idol. I carry multiple copies of the book with me to give out to friends."

For the past five years, Zach and I have regularly talked about his journey into generosity. His desire is to leverage his calling and assets to be strategic for the gospel globally.

Third-Generation Oil

Zach describes growing up in Texas. "I grew up in Marshall, Texas, during the 1970s and 1980s. My family was involved in oil exploration in Marshall dating back to the 1960s. My dad was a dentist by training. He went back to school and earned his doctorate in geology. In 1990 my family sold the company to Sonat, Inc. In 1993 our family and another family out of Kansas City, Missouri, purchased a package of oil and gas properties that was the foundation of a new company, Camterra Resources."

Zach attended Baylor University and completed an MBA degree at Southern Methodist University. He met his wife, Regan, in 1993, and they married in 1996. Zach grew up in the Methodist church in Marshall. He says, "I was impacted by two youth pastors who invested heavily in me." I have noticed how seriously Zach takes growing his faith. He has met regularly with a group of peers in the marketplace to challenge one another's growth.

Today Camterra Resources is valued at $150 million. Zach began as the company CFO in 2001 and has led the company since 2007, when he was thirty-four years old. Zach and Regan have three children.

A Vision for Generosity

Zach has reflected often on the significance of generosity in our conversations. "The more I give away the less I feel like a slave to the idols of money, comfort, and security. Every morning I try to declare before God that everything I have is ultimately his. I take the call to stewardship very seriously."

Reflecting on his relationship to Zandstra and Pine Cove Christian Camps, Zach speaks to the importance of Pine Cove's ministry to families. Pine Cove was established in 1964 and has grown into one of the largest Christian camps in the United States. Every summer more than fifty thousand children and their families attend there. Thousands of young people respond to the gospel, and many families see the intervention of God in marriages. One of the young people who experienced Christ at Pine Cove in her childhood was Leslie Doll (see chapter 3).

Zach was challenged to do something he had never done before. He made a $1 million pledge to Pine Cove. He describes his motivation. "Pine Cove is a special place that changes lives. There are so many broken families that experience the salvation and grace of God at this camp."

A Vision for New York City

Zach has the spiritual depth to grasp not only the strategic nature of investing in families but also investing in New York

City. He became one of the early investors in the New York City Movement Project, persuaded that this was an initiative of enormous strategic benefit to the globe.

Zach explains why he has been involved. "New York City is the most influential city in the world. I am convinced that if you can reach New Yorkers that they in turn will impact the world. I believe the highest rate of return on investment on a kingdom dollar is planting churches in global cities, starting in New York City. As a businessman, I want to invest my resources where I will see the greatest rate of return. Being involved with the NYC Movement Project has been enormously satisfying."

Zach also invested in Movement Day Global Cities, providing scholarships for international leaders. He believes the lessons learned in New York City from the past thirty years can create a laboratory for leaders and cities worldwide. This is a vision worth investing in.[1]

Isaiah and God's Vision

Isaiah's life and prophecy drew a correlation between vision and courage. The greater our vision of God, the greater our courage for God. Isaiah had the courage to persevere through four kingships in his prophetic role. May our vision, courage, and generosity reach others for four generations.

POINTS TO CONSIDER

1. God can work in the life of a younger marketplace leader to grapple with issues of financial idolatry, stewardship, and generosity.

2. Investing in families is an important building block of a godly society.
3. Cities like New York City are the tip of the spear for strategic philanthropy.

A PRAYER

Jesus, multiply the influence of younger, passionate marketplace leaders who will steward the next forty years of their lives to make an impact on the world. May there be a new movement of spiritually passionate and intellectually informed generosity to change the world. Amen.

18

Holding Fast

WHEN GRAHAM POWER STOPPED CHASING SUCCESS

> Maintain justice and do what is right, for my salvation is close at hand and my righteousness will soon be revealed. Blessed is the one who does this—the person who holds it fast, who keeps the Sabbath without desecrating it, and keeps their hands from doing any evil.
>
> Isaiah 56:1–2

In Isaiah 56 the prophet outlines what true spirituality looks like. He describes a people deeply committed to the promotion of justice as a sign of their true worship. The beneficiaries of this spirituality are the victims of injustice, the poor, and the homeless. Graham Power has been the embodiment of this spirituality for the past two decades.

Graham hosted me in his home one evening in April 2016. It was such an honor. I consider him to be one of the most effective Christian leaders of the past half century.

Growing Up Poor

Graham grew up in South Africa in the 1950s. His dad served in World War II as a mechanic. He had two siblings and finished high school at seventeen. Graham said of his mother, "My mom went to work on a bicycle so each of us children could afford to have shoes. My parents modeled sacrifice for us." Graham had a year of military training at the age of eighteen.

He joined a construction company and worked there for nine and a half years. By the age of twenty-one, he had become the youngest site manager, managing the construction of a hydroelectric dam. At twenty-eight, in 1983, he started his own construction company, Power Construction. He sold his home to purchase equipment. Graham said, "My father-in-law encouraged me to go out on my own. I started off with small projects—paving driveways, parking lots, and church property."

Over the next thirty years, Graham would see his company grow to two thousand employees as the one company had become twelve companies by 2007 (Power Group).

Graham explains why the company grew. "I believe that the growth of our company and the fact that we saw an exponential doubling of our turnover in the first five years was due to the quality of people that I surrounded myself with. Many of my colleagues from my first company indicated that they would count it an honor to join me should the opportunity present itself. These people had a desire to improve their status; they had a strong work ethic and were faithful. Interestingly, some of these people have been with Power since our inception."

Spiritual Poverty

Graham describes his spiritual journey. "I was chasing success. I was pursuing more boats, more game farms, more everything. Yet I could not find inner peace. At the end of 1998 I attended a Christian gathering at the Lord Charles Hotel. I had been invited dozens of times but rarely went.

"I ended up going and heard Michael Cassidy, the founder of African Enterprise, and I was challenged by his message. At a second gathering two months later, Peter Pollock spoke. He was one of the great cricket heroes in South Africa. He was an amazing evangelist and invited all of us to pray the sinner's prayer with him. Following this public commitment, I started to read the Bible daily, and two months later, while I was working through the Bible in my study, I was deeply touched. That evening, February 24, 1999, I committed my life unreservedly to Christ. I was forty-three years old. My wife, Lauren, would commit her life to Christ in an Alpha course."

The first thing Graham did was commit to clean up the corruption in his own company. He was gripped by Proverbs 11:1: "The LORD detests dishonest scales, but accurate weights find favor with him." He says, "That verse kept me up at night. The Bible says in Proverbs 20:17 that food that comes by fraud tastes sweet, but one ends up with a mouth full of gravel." Graham then contacted the fifteen other companies that had participated in tender collusion together and announced that he would no longer participate. This action represented a great risk to his company.

Two World-Changing Visions: Global Day of Prayer and Unashamedly Ethical

In 2000 Graham was on vacation in Spain when he woke up at 4:00 a.m. and saw a vision of a stadium filled with Christians from all denominations. They were gathering to pray and repent. He envisioned this starting in South Africa and spreading across the globe.

His vision included holding the gathering in a rugby stadium. The stadium agreed to allow the Global Day of Prayer (GDOP) to be birthed in 1999/2000 after twenty-two bombs exploded in Cape Town and a mafia style "war" was going on in the city.

Graham's team was told the largest prayer gathering in Cape Town to that point had been four thousand people. At the first gathering tickets were distributed for fifty thousand people. During that historic gathering people prayed for the racial divide, for political and church leadership, for people with HIV, and for the cessation of the bombings. The evening national television news gave extensive footage of the gathering, and the event was picked up on the front pages of South African newspapers.

In 2002 there were nine gatherings across South Africa, in 2003 the GDOP had spread to twenty-seven African nations, and in 2004 all fifty-six nations and islands in Africa participated (with an estimated twenty-two million people). In 2008 the gathering was planted in Jerusalem. In 2009 Hong Kong hosted the GDOP. In 2010 220 nations hosted the gathering (with an estimated 350 million people).

In October 2006 Graham was awakened again at 4:00 a.m. He says, "I felt electricity in my body. God showed me three waves that would sweep the globe. The first was a wave of prayer [GDOP]. The second was a wave of ethics, values, and clean living [Unashamedly Ethical]. Third, I saw a positive tsunami—a wave of revival and transformation like the world had never seen before. This was all rooted in the promise of God in 2 Chronicles 7:14 to hear our prayer, forgive our sin, and heal our land."

The Unashamedly Ethical movement began in response to rampant corruption in many developing regions—especially in Africa, South America, and India. Graham comments on the challenge. "Corruption in South Africa is endemic, and the global Corruption Perception Index shows that we have dropped twenty-seven places since 2001. Systemic corruption is like a cancer that is chewing away at the very core of our society, and the source is often greed and self-empowerment at the expense of others."[1]

Despite the challenges, the response has been overwhelming. In South Africa five thousand companies have taken the Unashamedly Ethical pledge and 112 nations are participating in this challenge (see www.unashamedlyethical.com).

In addition to these large, global visions, Graham is committed at a local level. For instance, he is involved in an upliftment initiative called Eagles Rising. For one year thirty black African students from the poorest townships are trained at and live on his farm, where they develop their English and computer literacy, Bible study, and life skills. When they finish at Eagles Rising, students are then assisted with finding employment or moving on to further their studies.

Graham attended Movement Day Global Cities, where the largest attending group was from South Africa. His presence served as an important validator that God is doing something special in our lifetime across the great cities of the globe.

Isaiah Held Fast

Isaiah held fast to God in difficult times. He did so with powerful admonitions to pray, repent, and perform justice. Holding fast is how we see God's work in the world. We see him creating global movements as his people hold fast together.

POINTS TO CONSIDER

1. God can work remarkably through someone who makes a wholehearted commitment to Christ later in life.
2. God can speak a vision into the life of a leader that can become a global movement.
3. Embodying what justice looks like at a local level gives credibility to a global message.

A PRAYER

Jesus, give us your vision for how we can reach our world and your world with expressions of justice. Let us start with united prayer, asking that our collective heart is aligned with yours. Amen.

19

Nobility

HOW DARIN AND PAULA OWEN
BECAME RECKLESS GIVERS

But the noble make noble plans, and by noble deeds
they stand.

Isaiah 32:8

In Isaiah 32 the prophet sketched out what a kingdom of righteousness looks like. He described noble persons as those who are generous, who have a heart that leans toward the poor and the disenfranchised. Righteousness, nobility, and generosity are the composite description of people who make a long-term difference in the lives of individuals, cities, and societies. Darin and Paula Owen have demonstrated that kind of nobility.

Over the past four years, Darin, his wife, Paula, and their two children have hosted me twice in their home in Durban, South Africa. I have found this couple to be two of the most generous people anywhere in regard to the entirety of their lives—their time, their resources, their home, and their passions.

Darin and his team, called City Story, built the largest international team to attend 2016 Movement Day Global Cities, with 150 leaders attending. In my observation, Durban may be the "Dallas of Africa," with such an extraordinary pool of Christian marketplace talent.

A Journey toward Christ

Darin's grandmother comes from a Jewish background. He told me, "When I was twenty-one years old, I had been working for a guy for six months and couldn't make any money. My dad encouraged me to take a risk and go on my own. He said I would always have a room in his home if things didn't work out. My dad constantly allowed homeless people to stay in the back of his business premises. When he died, it was amazing to see homeless persons come to the funeral. Excitingly for us, eighteen months before he died he came to faith in Christ."

Darin's own journey to Christ began when he was twenty-nine. His sister encouraged him to go and listen to a prophetic preacher in a local hotel. The preacher told Darin he envisioned him getting involved with lots of garments and fabric. Darin says, "I was not involved at that stage in any way with fabric or garments, as I was a builder. Two months later, by default, I was invited to make T-shirts for two stores. I ordered five hundred and immediately got into the clothing business full-time. Before long my company was making a million shirts. Within four months the prophecy had come to fruition. I went back to the pastor and committed my life to Christ." Darin is currently active in twelve companies.

Paula attended an Anglican high school as a boarder. She says, "I had always known about Christ but never served him until I attended the Alpha course. I was encouraged by my mom to get active in church. This took place when I was twenty-two years old." The Owens were married in 2001.

The Owens' Spiritual Passions

Paula describes her passion as serving families and children. This led to the birthing of an orphanage project in 2007 a few miles from their home outside of Durban. Paula says, "I have always felt the need to cross borders and break down barriers, including crossing language barriers." Over the next nine years, Paula would work toward building an orphanage both relationally as well as physically. Her colleague is Esther, another woman in the community. Esther's home became the hub of operations for the project. Paula and Esther started together by feeding two hundred children in the community every day.

After nine years, two homes have been built with staffing to care for twenty-four children. The homes provide food, clothing, and education, emulating a family unit. The next phase of the project is to build two more homes. Paula describes the need. "The father figures are completely missing. That presence is often provided by local pastors. The orphan population in South Africa is an estimated 3.7 million children. We are just scratching the surface but dream that our model can be replicated many times over. We are creating a manual to that end."

After his conversion, Darin attended Bible college for three years and had an idea of going into pastoral ministry. But he was challenged to stay in the marketplace and be Christ's person there. He led a marketplace ministry at his church for a decade.

After his Movement Day experience in New York City, he began to convene marketplace leaders in Durban. A group met to pray every Wednesday night for two hours. Every month a larger group would come to pray, with as many as five hundred people. In 2015 Darin brought a team of six couples to Movement Day in New York City.

Darin and his team forged a new organization in Durban— City Story. This has been instrumental in partnering with others in the city. One of those agencies is We Are Durban, which has recently brought seventy heads of nonprofits together. The purpose of the meetings is to ask them how they can be helped. These efforts have been mobilizing leaders for training purposes and forming relationships.

I was privileged to speak to 150 leaders at an April 2016 breakfast in Durban. There is extraordinary passion and talent in this network of Christ followers. I was fascinated to see the stirring in this part of South Africa, where so many powerful spiritual movements have been birthed in the past twenty years, including the Global Day of Prayer and the 2010 Cape Town Lausanne Congress. The Owens have a vision for the unity of the church in their city, the Christian marketplace community in their city, and for all of Africa.

I asked them about their philosophy of generosity. Paula responded, "When opportunity comes knocking on our door, we give at every opportunity. As a husband and wife, it has been a fun ride. It is something we can do together. It gives us the experience of unity as a couple."

Darin commented, "I want to be a reckless giver. If you sense the Spirit moving, you should put your check down. We have taken our entire savings account of 750,000 to 1,000,000 rand and emptied it out. What fun! I have seen that income return in six weeks! God keeps upping the ante. It is both scary and exciting at the same time. We have seen our giving increase from 10 percent to 92 percent of our income in certain years."[1]

Isaiah and the Nobility of God

Isaiah saw a kingdom of righteousness that would be led by people of nobility. Noble people commit to noble plans and noble deeds. When we are generous, we affirm the nobility of God and grow in our own nobility.

POINTS TO CONSIDER

1. Risk taking is important in our vocation as well as in our journey of generosity.
2. Building relationships among the poor is as important as assisting the poor financially.
3. The unity of the church in a city led by marketplace leaders is a powerful multiplier.

A PRAYER

Jesus, we are so glad that in your nobility you came to earth to perform the ultimate act of nobility—dying for us so we can emerge from our spiritual poverty. Amen.

20

Spending Yourselves

HOW HANNES VAN ASWEGAN
AND BOSHOFF GROBLER
REACHED OUT TO AFRICA'S POOR

If you spend yourselves in behalf of the hungry and
satisfy the needs of the oppressed, then your light
will rise in the darkness, and your night will become
like the noonday.

Isaiah 58:10

Isaiah introduced the idea of spending ourselves on behalf
of others who have nothing themselves to spend. He helps us
understand that we never become more like God than when
we spend ourselves for others. This is the gospel. God, in fact,
spent himself in the person of Christ so all our needs would
be satisfied—spiritual, physical, emotional, social. Though
he was rich for our sakes, he spent himself to the point of

spiritual bankruptcy so we would become infinitely rich. I have seen this truth played out in the lives of generous South African Christians.

South Africa has been an extraordinary crucible racially, politically, and spiritually. Nelson Mandela became the first black African to serve as president of the country. He served in that role from 1994 to 1999.

Against the backdrop of these enormous challenges, the Doxa Deo vision was birthed in 1996—a congregational movement that would create innovative efforts to address the challenges of their city, the city of Pretoria, and beyond. Critical to that movement was the engagement and involvement of senior marketplace leaders.

Hannes van Aswegan

Hannes van Aswegan was part of the 250-member South African delegation that came to New York City. We met over breakfast at the Jacob Javits Convention Center and had a subsequent phone interview to capture Hannes's spiritual journey against the backdrop of a changing South Africa.

Hannes grew up in a godly family in South Africa. He remembers his grandfather giving him a Bible for Christmas when he was eleven, with Psalm 37:5 inscribed inside: "Commit thy way unto the LORD, trust also in him; and he shall bring it to pass" (KJV). He was raised in the Dutch Reformed Church at a time when apartheid was the norm. Being a white South African Christian in the context of apartheid has always created dissonance for thoughtful Christians.

His father was a medical biophysicist, training radiologists and oncologists. Hannes's mother was a lecturer in communication sciences. Hannes ended up in the pharmaceutical field, and like his grandfather, he has been an entrepreneur, founding several health care–based companies since 2002. Hannes says, "The vision has always been to revolutionize the South African and then global health care environment.

"During the one-and-a-half-year period following the launch of our first start-up, we went through several challenges typical to the start-up scene, especially regarding cash flow. I found myself investigating several options including 'full-time ministry,' which lead to me enrolling in Bible school. I now realize that I am in full-time ministry. Matthew 6:33 really spoke to me about seeking God first in all things."

I asked Hannes what his passions are. He said, "I want to help Christian businesspeople understand why they are in business. I want to see Christian unity among the marketplace Christian community. We can achieve so much together in a challenging environment like South Africa."[1]

Working toward this passion, Hannes has joined other business people at Doxa Deo to lead the business ministry for a collection of congregations in Pretoria and is engaging other churches to create city-changing momentum. This is being done by establishing the importance of calling and purpose in Christian businesspeople's lives.

Hannes and his wife, Lizel, also share a passion for bridging the gap between different races and cultures in the South African landscape. They find great fulfillment in being active in the leadership of the first racially integrated congregation of Doxa Deo, and they are actively mentoring young, passionate Christian leaders of different cultures.

As a follow-up to the Movement Day Global Cities experience, Hannes is part of a planning team with Jurie Kriel and other African leaders to bring a Movement Day expression to multiple African cities.

Boshoff Grobler

Boshoff Grobler was born into a middle-class South African family and had four siblings. His father was a secondhand car salesman and his mother was a social worker. He remembers, "When my mom died, I saw these disheveled people at her funeral. They were the ones she had invested in, and they felt the need to be there."

In our interview, Boshoff commented that he grew up with a strong sense of calling to change the lives of people around him. He made a faith commitment at the age of eleven. He says, "Though I did not grow up with very much, I felt the need to become a change agent. I view generosity not primarily in monetary terms, but what I give my energy to and how I effect energy in others."

Boshoff serves as the CEO of Ashburton Investments. Their purpose is described on their website.

> Ashburton Investments was formed during 2012 to become the African based non-traditional asset manager of choice for African and corridor clients. The new business was established after a comprehensive strategy review of FirstRand's capabilities and the opportunities that were offered because of the Global Financial Crisis.[2]

Boshof describes where he prioritizes his energies.

1. **Family**—"It is incredibly important to get a life partner that shares your passions," Boshoff says. "My wife and I have a deep passion for marriages in our country. The divorce rate is extraordinary. We started marriage counseling camps by buying a property and teaming up with partners providing monthly retreats for couples. We have had many couples come with divorce papers and become healed in Christ at the camp. We tithe a net of our assets to the camp ministry."

2. **Youth**—Boshoff is involved in the youth ministry of his church. He and Lizel are involved with children ages eighteen months to six years. His own children—who were nine, eleven, and eighteen at the time of our interview—sometimes teach with them. Their passions intersect in one place.

3. **Financial Management**—"In Africa," Boshoff says, "the net household savings rate is below zero. We are seeing an increase in household income but no savings. Those who are saving are saving inefficiently. In the United States people are saving to retire on 64 percent of their income. In South Africa the people saving are saving at 12 percent of their income. The goals are to get more people to save, those that are saving to do it more efficiently, and to get more hard currency into Africa."

4. **Serving Doxa Deo**—"Our church is a powerful change agent," Boshoff says. "We function in our church not as a huddle, but to drive change.[3]

Isaiah and the Poor

One of the great themes of Isaiah is to spend one's self on behalf of the poor. The lives of the poor are enriched and dignified, and the person spending him- or herself becomes a great light in a dark and violent world.

POINTS TO CONSIDER

1. Awakening marketplace leaders to their callings is a high and holy assignment.

2. Gifted marketplace leaders are called to intersect the felt needs of their cities.

3. Managing one's energy is extraordinarily strategic, and aligning that energy with God-given passions multiplies one's impact.

A PRAYER

Jesus, use the gifted marketplace men and women of South Africa to make an impact on the great needs of their country. Out of the great crucible of suffering, continue to raise up leaders who will influence the world through their great energy and effectiveness. Amen.

21

Good News

BOB AND TRACIE EDMISTON SHARE A GOD-SIZED VISION

The Spirit of the Sovereign LORD is on me, because the LORD has anointed me to proclaim good news to the poor.

Isaiah 61:1

At the heart of Isaiah's vision is a Messiah who would bring good news to the poor. The good news—or the gospel—is the heart of God's message of salvation to the world.

Given the fact that the world population is growing exponentially, the message of salvation to the whole world is more urgent than ever. One agency that takes that reality as seriously as any is Christian Vision, founded by Bob Edmiston. This is the story of Bob and his wife, Tracie.

Bob's Story

Bob and I met in May 2016 in Birmingham, England, at the corporate offices of IM Group. Raymond Harris and Ram Gidoomal of London joined us (see chapters 4 and 12).

He was born in India in 1946, one year before that country gained its independence from the British. His parents met during World War II. His dad was a pilot fighting the Japanese, and when he broke his nose he met a nurse who became his wife. Bob left India in 1949 at the age of three, traveled to the UK, and then moved to Africa at the age of ten. He moved back to the UK in 1962.

Bob grew up Roman Catholic. His father was not part of his faith journey, though he became interested in spiritual things later in life. Bob says, "I had a bad impression of God growing up. He didn't seem real to me. After returning to England at age seventeen, I began to attend a youth meeting in a small church, in Essex, of thirty members. After six months, I understood that Jesus died for me, and I began to follow Jesus."

Bob had the early impression that God had spoken to him, saying, "You will stand before kings." That impression was initially interpreted as a missionary calling to Africa, but that did not materialize. Bob has always been keen in telling others about his beliefs but found it difficult, especially in the early years in Britain.

He started work as a bank clerk, later qualifying as an accountant. He got his first top-level job in an automobile business, and at the age of twenty-seven he began work at Jensen Motors as financial controller, out of an applicant list of one hundred. The company went bankrupt after the car industry was disrupted by the global 1973 oil crisis, but they still had many auto parts in inventory. Jensen Parts and Services was formed out of the ashes of that bankruptcy.

The company evolved into an auto import business and over time was renamed International Motors. It also added additional lines of business, including property, and the name was changed to IM Group. It has subsidiaries including Isuzu and Subaru distribution. In 1988 Bob became full owner at the age of forty-two.

Tracie's Story

Tracie was born in England into a Christian family. Her older brother became a pastor, and she was raised in an Assembly of God church. Tracie was very active in leadership at her church prior to meeting Bob. She ran the children's ministry, taught Sunday school, and led worship. She left school at sixteen to take up a commercial apprenticeship and do business studies. Tracie describes herself as a "people addict," always involved with many people. When you meet Tracie, you realize how infectious her enthusiasm can be. At the age of nineteen she left the telecommunications world to live closer to the church and work as a volunteer.

The UK government put funding toward organizations to help with those experiencing long-term unemployment. Tracie entered the project and became its secretary, then a supervisor and manager. The project turned into eighty people, which helped the disabled and underprivileged. By the age of twenty-two, Tracie had become its manager, and she realized the church could share the gospel by going into the community at their greatest point of need.

Christian Vision

When Tracie turned twenty-five, the government changed the program, and she felt the need to move in a different direction. Bob, who had met Tracie since they were now attending the same church, asked if she would be interested in helping him start

Christian Vision. Tracie began her role as managing director at the inception of Christian Vision in December 1988. The Edmistons were married ten years later in 1998.

Christian Vision began as an initiative to share the gospel with one billion people worldwide through modern communication methods. Thirty years later, there are now twenty-seven offices around the world, with teams creating innovative ways to share the gospel. The Christian Vision website simply says, "Our Vision—we are a global Christian ministry with a strategic goal to reach a billion people with the Gospel."[1]

In Latin America, Christian Vision collaborated with 550 FM radio stations. A television station was started and passed over to Boas Novas Brasil. On-the-ground projects have been established across Africa, Myanmar, and Venezuela. Over time the strategy evolved into an internet-based methodology.

The Edmistons say, "Our vision is to impact one billion people. We are pushing forward in exploring every opportunity, especially using the internet. Our measurement is in souls converted. In the past month, there were 650,000 visits to our landing pages. There were 250,000 validated users of Yes He Is—a mobile phone app to help persons use the internet to share their faith. The purpose is to initiate conversations to do the work of evangelism." In addition to the internet evangelism strategy, Christian Vision has funded one thousand missionaries (at one time) doing pioneer work within their own countries.

In addition to his leadership in business and Christian mission, Bob has influenced Britain politically. He has been a member of the Conservative Party, and on November 19, 2010, it was announced that he would be created a Life Peer—formally introduced to the House of Lords on January 11, 2011. He sat as a Conservative in the House of Lords with the title Baron Edmiston of Lapworth in the County of Warwickshire. He was appointed by the queen, and recommended by the prime minister, to the House of Lords. He retired from the House of Lords in July 2015. The word from God about speaking to kings and queens had come true.

A September 2016 article in the *Sunday Times* stated that Bob Edmiston had become the first Christian evangelical billionaire in the United Kingdom. The IM Group was particularly profitable in 2015 when profits soared to £149 million. The Birmingham business has net tangible assets of £993 million, per the article.[2]

I asked the Edmistons about the principles that have guided their philanthropy and engagement. They reflected, "God is not impressed with wealth. One soul is more important than all the wealth in the world. We subscribe to the Bible passage that to whom much is given, much is expected. You can't take it with you, but you can send it ahead."[3]

The Edmistons have a high view of the body of Christ. Their commitment is to work with other kingdom-minded leaders and agencies. Their passion is to see those who come to faith planted in local churches where they can grow spiritually. They believe every part of the body is important.

Isaiah and the Lost

Just as Isaiah prophesied about the coming of Jesus as the Great Evangelist, today innovative efforts like Christian Vision are sharing the gospel with the multitudes. Jesus came to seek and save the lost that none should perish.

POINTS TO CONSIDER

1. God can provide a word of destiny to us at an early age.
2. The worth of one soul is greater than all the wealth in the world.

3. It takes the whole body of Christ to reach and disciple the masses.

A PRAYER

Jesus, you care for every person in the world. Use every means necessary and every person available to share yourself with everyone on the globe. Amen.

22

Gospel

WAYNE ("JUNIOR") HUIZENGA JR.
AND WAYNE COTTON'S IMPACTFUL FRIENDSHIP

> He was pierced for our transgressions.
>
> Isaiah 53:5

Isaiah 53 has been described as the clearest presentation of the gospel in the Old Testament. Many Jewish Christians point to this passage as a major turning point in their spiritual journey. It is the heart of the gospel—that Jesus was pierced for our transgressions, that he died for our sins. That truth can melt the heart of the most hardened skeptic of the gospel.

The gospel became real to both Wayne Huizenga Jr. ("Junior" to his friends) and Wayne Cotton as adults. Their story of friendship is one of sharing the gospel through the enormous influence God has given them.

We met in Junior's office in Palm Beach, Florida, on May 2, 2016. He is CEO of Rybovich Marina, which provides service to the yachting community. On the wall was a photograph of Beach-Fest in South Florida, which took place in March 2003. The aerial photo captures an estimated 250,000 attendees who listened to evangelist Luis Palau. BeachFest in South Florida and Billy Graham speaking to 250,000 in New York City's Central Park in 1991 are the two largest gatherings in American evangelicalism's history.

Wayne and Junior had become friends in 2001, and together they cochaired the BeachFest outreach in 2003. The two men brought their Christian faith and business acumen together to achieve one of the greatest outreaches in American church history. I met Wayne at a Movement Day gathering in New York City in 2013. He was inspired by the potential of continuing to link Christian businessmen with faith leaders in cities.

Lives Disrupted

Wayne was born in New Jersey in 1954 and moved to Florida when he was two. Junior was born in 1961. Both sets of parents divorced when their sons were five years old. For Junior that meant moving back to Illinois, where his family had Dutch roots. He lived there until he was thirteen, but he visited Florida in the summer and saw his family then.

Both sides of their families struggled to get by. Junior says, "My mom had to manage three jobs for us to survive." Wayne says, "My mom juggled two jobs for us to get by."

Both Wayne and Junior had significant Christian influences in their lives. Junior's grandparents would take him to church. Wayne was partially influenced by a Presbyterian church growing up and attended church in college and the Evangelism Explosion class.

Wayne met his wife, Doretta, when he was attending Broward Community College and she was attending Florida Bible

College. They were married in 1977 when Wayne was working in the flooring industries. He has served as president of Designed Flooring Distributors for thirty-two years and joined American OEM on the manufacturing side in 2014.

In 1979 Wayne was in a violent car crash. He says, "A truck tire came through my car windshield. The car collapsed and I had to be removed with the 'jaws of life.'" After the accident, Wayne had extensive surgery to rebuild his hands. One of the hospital visitors told his mom, "He's not alone." This brush with death was a defining moment for him spiritually, and he began to deeply engage in his faith.

Fortune 500 Companies

Junior's father, Wayne Huizenga Sr., became the first person in American history to create three Fortune 500 companies. Waste Management became a public company in 1972, and by 1983 it had become the largest waste disposal company in the United States. Blockbuster began in 1987 and became the nation's largest movie rental company by 1994. AutoNation was founded in 1996 and became the nation's largest automotive dealer. Huizenga Sr. has been a five-time recipient of *Financial World* magazine's "CEO of the Year" award. His ownerships have also included the Miami Dolphins, Florida Panthers, and Florida Marlins.

Junior began his work career as a stock boy at Blockbuster. He told me, "When our Blockbuster stock was sold, we became very wealthy overnight. It opened up a very new chapter in our lives."

Junior met Fonda, his future wife, in Florida when he was fifteen. He describes a pivotal point later on in his spiritual journey. "By this time I was married with children, and my mother challenged me to raise them with some sort of grounding and recommended I return to church. I told her I didn't have the time for church—I was partying on the weekends and engaging in excessive drinking. I took her words more seriously, however, after meeting Navy Captain Brad McDonald, who frequently accompanied me on fishing trips."

After spending three years getting to know McDonald, Junior decided he wanted to be more like him. That's when the captain suggested a relationship with Christ. After attending a few different churches, Junior says, he truly accepted Christ. He repented during an altar call at a megachurch when a pastor told him he believed God had a purpose for his life. Junior stood in front of 3,500 people and accepted Christ that day. His mother later fell gravely ill and died, but his faith allowed him to care for her in a way he would not have been able to before meeting Christ. That was in 2001.

BeachFest

The seeds of BeachFest were sown through a meeting Wayne had with Stephen Palau in 1998. Palau was a teacher at Wayne's children's school in Florida. Through that connection, Wayne met Luis Palau, Stephen's brother.

Wayne and Junior met through mutual friends. Junior says, "Wayne became a role model for the kind of man I wanted to be. His teenage children raised our children. I wanted my children to learn from godly young people."

Shortly after his conversion, Junior began to share his testimony in public. In 2002 he spoke at Christian businessman's meeting. The meeting was attended by a small group of CEOs. As Junior was becoming active in sharing his faith, he and Wayne decided to team up to cochair BeachFest, working with Luis Palau.

As BeachFest took shape, Wayne and Junior brought their very significant networks to bear on the event. Junior engaged players from the Miami Dolphins to assist with promotion and the program. As the 2003 event was approaching, God was doing some remarkable things in both of their families.

Junior recounts, "I have the photograph of my dad being on stage at BeachFest and praying to receive Christ during that outreach. He was very involved in assisting us to involve others with the event. My son and daughter also came to faith at BeachFest."

Wayne says, "There were trainings across the state. We involved more than twelve thousand volunteers. We believe there were more than nine thousand responses to the gospel during the two-day outreach. We were given one report that as many as five hundred thousand people participated in the two days."[1]

The Fruit of BeachFest

After the 2003 outreach, several new efforts were birthed. The National Christian Foundation of South Florida was created. This has helped to pool philanthropic resources for Christian outreach in Florida and beyond.

Life Work Leadership was also created. This nine-month course creates a cohort of marketplace leaders who meet monthly to sharpen each other as peers. The program introduces participants to a world-class faculty, who create an alumni base of committed Christian marketplace leaders. The program has been replicated in other cities across the United States.

The Huizengas have also been deeply involved in the foster care system. Their philanthropy has been used to stimulate the engagement of families with children needing foster care.

Both Junior and Wayne have maintained significant involvement with the Luis Palau Association. The LPA has been active in stimulating gospel expressions in cities around the world through service and proclamation.

Isaiah and the Gospel

In Isaiah 53, Isaiah gave us the greatest picture of the gospel in the entire Old Testament. With stunning accuracy, he portrayed what would happen 750 years in the future: Jesus would come to be pierced in our place. He would die our death and put death to death.

POINTS TO CONSIDER

1. God can redeem the deep places of brokenness in people's lives by making them sensitive to the gospel.
2. Christian marketplace leaders have networks and acumen significantly needed to make an impact in cities and regions.
3. The power of a collaborative Christian friendship such as Wayne and Junior's could significantly affect a huge region and create a compelling global model through that friendship.

A PRAYER

Jesus, thank you for raising up businessmen and businesswomen to be at the forefront of sharing the gospel with their peers. Thank you for so radically redeeming lives that result in a powerful and compelling witness. Multiply this witness in the great global cities of the world. Amen.

23

Justice

IVAN HINRICHS'S CALL TO STEWARDSHIP

> Learn to do right; seek justice. Defend the oppressed.
> Take up the cause of the fatherless; plead the case
> of the widow.
>
> Isaiah 1:17

At the beginning of his prophecy, Isaiah announced God's expectation for his people—he wanted them to know his heart for the fatherless and the oppressed. The Bible consistently proclaims this as a standard of our discipleship. James announced that true religion is caring for the widow and the orphan.

I have seen this modeled in a community of friends in Charlotte, North Carolina. This community is passionate about impacting the fatherless and the widow. One of those friends is Bishop Claude Alexander.

Claude is an extraordinarily impressive leader. He has led his Charlotte congregation, The Park Church, which has eight thousand attendees, for twenty-five years. He has served as the president of the Hampton's Minister's Conference, which represents perhaps the largest clergy body in the world. The conference, which meets every June, is predominantly African American.

Claude came to our second Movement Day event in Dallas. He has become one of our great proponents for the spread of Movement Day to other cities in the United States and globally. He said in an interview at the National Discussion on Race, "Movement Day brings muscularity to the expression of the church in a city. That is why I am a champion for its expression in Charlotte."[1]

During my first visit to Charlotte in 2016, I met Ivan Hinrichs at a luncheon hosted by our mutual friend Claude. Ivan is a longtime member of Myers Park Presbyterian Church in Charlotte, along with Leighton Ford, brother-in-law to Billy Graham.

A Cross-Cultural Journey

While growing up in Texas, Ivan made a faith commitment at a Southern Baptist church. He was a second grader. In his teens, he became more rebellious. He comments, "My parents decided spending summers on my uncle's farm in Kansas was a good idea. I loved it. For four summers I worked six days a week from ten to fourteen hours a day. This gave me time to think things through. I remember listening to Billy Graham's *Hour of Decision* every Sunday night. That was spiritually impactful for me."

In high school Ivan traveled to Europe as the result of winning a *Parade* magazine contest. He saw the pope—as well as Gina Lollobrigida! After seeing the destruction of Pompeii, Ivan was reminded of the book of Ecclesiastes—and how everything has a season. His world was widening.

Ivan received his university training at Wheaton College, where he met his wife, Evelyn. He discovered he had an aptitude for sales and decided to make a career in insurance. The couple landed in Charlotte in 1965, where they were married. Once in Charlotte, Ivan called Leighton Ford, whom he had heard speak in a Wheaton chapel service. Ford encouraged them to attend Myers Park Presbyterian Church.

Ivan's career in the insurance world led him to work with Connecticut Mutual, which became Mass Mutual in 1996. He developed what he called a "benefits boutique company" that served highly compensated executives. Ivan has been an agent, supervisor, assistant general agent, and general agent. His agency led Connecticut Mutual in production for fourteen years and Mass Mutual Disability Income production for ten years.

I asked Ivan what his primary spiritual passion is. He said, in one word, "Stewardship." He further commented, "I have been in the middle of so much family estate planning that I see the importance of planning ahead and being strategic. I have interacted with several pastors and church leaders—most of whom have very little understanding or training on steward-ship. My passion is to help pastors understand that they are not fund-raisers for their church but rather training a congregation of stewards who are trustees of all that God has entrusted to them. If a pastor can train his congregation well, fund-raising will take care of itself."

CrossRoads

One of the Charlotte stewardship projects the Hinrichs and his congregation are involved with is the CrossRoads Corporation.

CrossRoads was founded in 2008 by Don Gately and Neil Mc-Bryde as the result of a church capital campaign. The campaign raised $32 million dollars with 40 percent committed to outreach. From that funding, CrossRoads was established as a 501(c)(3) with a seed grant of $1.5 million.

CrossRoads is focused on working with the Grier Heights neighborhood for community revitalization. The vision is that Grier Heights will be transformed residentially and economically. The working teams are focused on six areas:

New homes—Building twenty-three homes on the lots of people from mixed-income backgrounds

Critical home repair—Partnering with Habitat for Humanity, helping existing homeowners stay in their homes. Twelve homes have been assisted.

Youth programs—In Grier Heights, 40 percent of the population is under eighteen. Youth programs keep young people off the streets by providing after-school, literacy, and swimming lessons.

Early childhood education—The most crucial factor in breaking a cycle of poverty for young people is for them to graduate from high school. If children start kindergarten behind, they are two-and-a-half-times more likely to drop out of school. The program provides tuition-free training for one hundred preschool students.

Community center—After taking possession of an original schoolhouse, the center is providing training courses in computers, high school equivalency, and overall job preparedness.

Stay in Fellowship team—Given the racial divides in Charlotte, this is an effort to get people together through book studies, movie discussions, and workshops.

The work of CrossRoads is grounded in two principles: (1) do "with" and not "for" the poor; partnership must be done in concert with the community, and (2) leverage through partnerships rather than just building a large staff team. The Habitat partnership is a great model for this.

In nine years, the partnership has attracted $7 million in funding through this unique approach. CrossRoads has been recognized as one of the two most effective nonprofits in Charlotte.[2]

The work of CrossRoads is a model of what Movement Day wants to incubate and promote. I asked Ivan why he was involved with Movement Day. He responded, "I am captured by the vision, as modeled by Paul's ministry in the New Testament, to meet the needs of a city. Breaking down silos and opening passageways between different churches with an understanding of what each other is doing is critical. Movement Day creates a means for leaders to talk to each other about the greatest needs of their cities. Movement Day has the same spirit of Billy Graham's ministry in being able to stick to the core themes of Jesus's ministry and draw very diverse congregations together. If Movement Day can impact Charlotte, it will be a sign of hope for all of urban America."

Kingdom Investors

Ivan commented on how kingdom investors can be more effective. "Mechanics matter. I encourage investors to use donor-advised giving accounts. It is important to set a cap on one's lifestyle to have the maximum amount of funding to invest in a kingdom cause. For our family, this worked and we can give away 60 percent of our income. This allows us to invest significantly in my church as well as in Gordon-Conwell; Salvation Army; Charlotte Rescue Mission; Habitat for Humanity; Fellowship of Christian Athletes; and in our missionary, Ben Page, living in Grier Heights; and in Movement Day."[3]

Isaiah and Justice

A predominant theme in Isaiah's writings is justice for the poor and justice in the city context. One of God's primary attributes is that he is just. God calls for his people to exercise justice toward the poor and the disadvantaged, as illustrated in the Grier Heights story.

POINTS TO CONSIDER

1. Effective financial stewardship can multiply the impact of a single life in multiple causes.
2. Crossing racial lines is an important priority in building an environment for justice.
3. Biracial friendships can be extraordinarily fruitful in bringing hope to a troubled city.

A PRAYER

Jesus, you achieved the justice of God by dying on the cross for us. As you have become our Advocate, may we advocate on behalf of those who are disadvantaged and helpless. Amen.

24

Praying

ROBERT LEVY'S JOURNEY IN JAMAICA

> You who call on the LORD, give yourselves no rest.
>
> Isaiah 62:6

In Isaiah 62 God describes watchmen being posted on Jerusalem's walls. The image is one of a community of intercessors who cry out to the Lord day and night for his purposes to be fulfilled. I believe God puts into our hearts the very themes he wants us to pray for—a divine mystery we are invited into. Our praying aligns with the holy passion God puts deep within us. This is modeled in the life of Robert Levy.

I met Robert on May 12, 2016, at Movement Day in Port-au-Prince, Haiti. He and his colleague, Richard Sadler, had flown from Kingston, Jamaica, to join us at the Montana Hotel for our first Haiti Movement Day. Robert serves as chairman of Jamaica Broilers, one of the largest employers in the entire Caribbean.

May 12 was a significant day—exactly sixty-four months after the great Haitian earthquake. The Montana Hotel had been destroyed that day of January 12, 2010, and it was a perfect metaphor for our gathering—to see God accelerate a spiritual movement across the islands to rebuild lives among the deep spiritual and social needs of the Caribbean people.

Robert spoke on "The Greatest Movement Day in History," and reflected on the three greatest empires in history: the Babylonian Empire, the Medo-Persian Empire, and the Roman Empire. In each of these historic periods, God had men and women like Daniel and Esther, who changed the course of history with their spiritual leadership.

Early Days

In our interview, Robert reflected on other "Daniels" in history who have been God's voice during the reign of great empires, such as Wesley, Whitefield, and Wilberforce in the British Empire. Robert is conscious of world history. His ancestors were of Jewish ancestry from Spain, and they relocated to Jamaica after the Spanish Inquisition, which began in 1478. Over the centuries, the Levy family intermarried with other Caribbean residents.

Robert's father was in the poultry business and import business starting in the 1950s. Jamaica Broilers officially organized in 1958, and the family was relatively affluent.

Robert told me, "I grew up with two problems. I am accident prone. I lost two fingers, one on each hand. Secondly, I was born with dyslexia. Thus, learning was difficult and I dropped out of high school. Despite these challenges, I had everything a young man could want, including a house on the golf course."

He went on to describe himself as a "dirty fellow," arrogant, in the 1970s. He planned to leave the company, and he gave his dad two months' notice.

At that time his mother had become a follower of Jesus, but he and his father were spiritually uninterested. Then, Robert says, "I told the Lord, 'Take over my life. Give me peace and everything will be right.' I sat in the church for hours searching for peace." On the day he was leaving the company, he locked his office door, crying out to God once more. God said, "How can I do anything with your life until it's surrendered to me?" That was the moment of spiritual reckoning, and Robert was converted, becoming a follower of Jesus.

He describes a season of tremendous spiritual growth. "I attended the Jamaica Bible College in Mandeville, which had become like Keswick, a great Bible conference center in England. I got involved with great Christian men. I was trained by graduates of Dallas Theological Seminary and Navigators. Two years later my dad and my brother became Christians, in the mid-1970s."

Jamaica Broilers

Robert rejoined the company with his father in the early 1980s, and the company began a makeover. He took to heart the admonition: "Your life is going to count in proportion to your time in Scripture." He says, "I have been able to read the Bible through twenty times, writing notes on every chapter in the Bible."

The Lord redeemed Robert's educational path by giving him exceptional wisdom regarding the use of the computer, which helped him improve his grammar. He was invited in the 1980s to attend the Harvard Business School's Owner/President Management course for those leaders who manage more than

$100 million in revenue a year. Robert would attend a month a year for three years. The company had come a long way since the first three investors in the 1950s had each contributed $5,000. Robert never would have dreamed he would have an educational opportunity at Harvard after dropping out of high school.

He describes a financial turning point in the company's history. "Just before the year 2000, the company had been carrying $20 million in debt. I gathered our core team every Thursday to pray for ninety minutes for help with our financial management. Eight of us prayed for eighteen months, and in two years our cash position improved to $20 million in cash with no debt."

Robert has led the company to an explicitly based mission as stewards of God's resources. The company's mission statement on its website reads:

> With God's guidance, we will efficiently manage the company to fulfill our obligations to our customers, shareholders, employees, contractors and the community at large, with an attitude of service and a commitment to truth, fairness and the building of goodwill.[1]

Jamaica Broilers had a 2015 gross revenue of $400 million with two thousand employees in Jamaica and three hundred employees in the United States. The company manages 70 percent of the poultry business in Jamaica.

As Jamaica Broilers turned fifty years old in 2008, they celebrated by hosting a Luis Palau Festival in Jamaica. Every year Jamaica Broilers has hosted a festival in Jamaica or Haiti as an evangelistic outreach to cities across the Caribbean. In 2016 seventy thousand people attended the Fun in the Son Festival in Kingston, with three thousand recorded responses to the gospel.

One of Robert's daughters married Andrew Palau, Luis's son. Robert's other daughter married Christian artist TobyMac.

Robert's son Christopher is president of Jamaica Broilers, and his other son, Stephen, runs the United States operation. Robert and his wife have been married more than fifty years.

I asked him what spiritual principles have guided his leadership and philanthropy. He said, "We are living in a time where Judeo-Christian principles and lifestyles are under the greatest attack ever. Every effort must be made for large impact, and Movement Days like today are so important for bringing the church together for empowerment and encouragement. This will become more and more relevant as the enemy increases his attack."[2]

Isaiah and the Command to Pray

In Isaiah 62:6–7 the Lord commands his people to "give yourselves no rest, and give him no rest till he establishes Jerusalem and makes her the praise of the earth." This passage catalyzed the Moravian movement of the eighteenth century, which brought revival to Europe and Christianity to the United States. The Moravians prayed every day for a century toward the purposes of this prayer. May God do the same across all our cities.

POINTS TO CONSIDER

1. God is working through the centuries to position people to reach modern-day empires through their business acumen and spiritual leadership.
2. God can redeem educational and family challenges to bring people to himself.
3. God can raise up successful businesses and leaders to create a powerful citywide and regional witness.

A PRAYER

Jesus, you are our Great High Priest. Use our prayers to initiate a great revival in our respective cities as marketplace leaders and ministry leaders evangelize their communities around the world. Amen.

25

Rising Sun

GARY KINNAMAN, BILLY THRALL, BRAD EDSON, BRET EDSON, AND DALE MARR: SHARING A COMMON MISSION

> From the west, people will fear the name of the LORD, and from the rising of the sun, they will revere his glory.
>
> Isaiah 59:19

Isaiah saw a new day when nations would fall in reverence before the Lord. Over the centuries, the knowledge of the Lord would permeate the whole earth. Nations and tribes who formally had no meaningful contact with the gospel would be drawn to God's salvation.

Phoenix, Arizona, is a city drawing people from around the world. It has grown dramatically in recent decades through both immigration and migration. In that context God has raised up a community of leaders who are bringing the diverse tribes in God's kingdom together.

Gary Kinnaman

I was introduced to Phoenix through Gary Kinnaman. Gary came to our first Movement Day gathering in New York City in 2010. He is a remarkable leader, having pastored one of the Phoenix megachurches for more than two decades. His leadership spans a breadth of involvements, including writing books, helping to build a network of the largest churches in Phoenix, and interfacing with the Catholic Church through his American Bible Society assignment. Gary and his wife, Marilyn, have made their home my home when I've stayed in Phoenix.

Gary has introduced me to several extraordinary leaders across the greater Phoenix region. Phoenix is the largest city geographically in the United States and the sixth largest by population. My observation is that Phoenix may have the most well-connected megachurch network of any major city in the United States. The fruit of that connection has resulted in several innovative campaigns, including CityServe and HopeFest.

Churches like Central Christian Church led by Cal Jernigan and Christ's Church of the Valley led by Don Williams have been extraordinarily influential in Phoenix. More than twenty-five pastors of large churches have been knit together for a decade. Remarkable networks of emerging churches exist as well as a robust network of Hispanic leaders.

Gary introduced me to four leaders who have influenced the city for the past three decades—Billy Thrall, Brad and Bret Edson, and Dale Marr.

Billy Thrall

Billy grew up in Phoenix and pastored an inner-city urban church for two decades. He and his wife, Charlotte, have had a tremendous heart to help the poor and disenfranchised. Billy and Charlotte were asked to start HopeFest when it launched.

HopeFest has annually served more than twenty thousand people through its vision to serve the underserved, the uninsured, and underresourced of Phoenix all on the same day. Services have included medical, dental, and vision, as well as several other practical resources. More than fifty agencies and companies have cosponsored HopeFest, and it has married the efforts of the church to share the gospel and be the gospel through acts of kindness.

Billy serves as the executive director for Movement Day Arizona, and Grand Canyon University served as the first host site in September 2017. The school is one of the fastest-growing universities in the world, with a campus population of more than nineteen thousand students and an online student body of more than sixty thousand.

Brad and Bret Edson

Two Phoenix friends introduced to me early on were brothers Bret and Brad Edson. The Edsons' office in downtown Phoenix served as a hub for many of the major faith-based activities across Phoenix.

The Edsons created Marketplace One after selling the family business a decade ago, and Leadership X Events began in 2008 as an initiative of Marketplace One. The partners understand the tension inherent to living out their Christian calling in the marketplace. Past presenters have included Tim Keller, Kurt Warner, and Eric Metaxas.

From the Marketplace One website:

> As an experimental think tank, our mission is to promote the ideas and encourage the leaders that create gospel-centered ventures for the glory of God and the common good.
>
> We believe that God calls people to serve society with the talents they have been given, and that many are called to exercise their giftedness in the context of the marketplace.
>
> For one reason or another, however, high-capacity Christian marketplace leaders are an underserved demographic. We therefore seek to identify, develop, and partner with key leaders who have the capacity to make a positive impact in society.[1]

Due to growth and demand, the One Institute is now an independent 501(c)(3) organization that serves marketplace leaders across the United States. Brian Mackay provides leadership to the One Institute.[2] The Edsons have hosted many of the initial meetings to launch Movement Day Arizona. They represent a neutral and trusted voice for the region.

Dale Marr

Gary also introduced me to Dale Marr. Dale has been in the construction industry for thirty-five years. He describes growing up in Illinois and moving to Arizona. "I grew up in Illinois in a family that was not particularly spiritual. I met Christ toward the end of my high school years while dating Susie, whom I would eventually marry. I was attracted to the diversity and high adventure offered in the West, and finished my civil engineering degree at the University of Arizona."

For the past fifteen years, Dale has been one of the owners of Concord General Contracting, with his firm earning between $50 and $55 million in annual revenue. The firm employs forty-five people. Over the past twenty years, Concord has assisted more than ninety churches in renovating and building their church campuses. The network was facilitated through Gary's relationship with the broader network of Arizona churches, and Dale has been delighted to assist Phoenix churches of every size and shape.

The Marr family has had broad mission involvement. Dale says, "We have taken several short-term mission trips with friends and family. Susie is a physical therapist. We have particularly enjoyed being involved with Joni and Friends' work with the disabled community. We both want to serve the needs of others locally and globally."

Dale has agreed to join a community of business leaders as a board of reference for Movement Day Arizona. I asked him about his involvement with Gary, Billy, and Movement Day Arizona. He said, "Movement Day is appealing to me because it brings all of the spokes of the wheel together for God's church in a city. It is extremely powerful to see churches, agencies, and marketplace leaders to create more cohesion. When there is more cohesion, there is more power."[3]

Isaiah and Service

Isaiah's prophecy included a time in history when people of all nations would be drawn to the beauty and power of the Lord. This is happening as never before in world history as the nations are coming into the neighborhoods of the world. As the body of Christ serves the nations in our neighborhoods, the aroma of Christ is released.

POINTS TO CONSIDER

1. Citywide networks built over decades of faithful leadership will bear enormous fruit in the life of a city.

2. Uniting the church in a complex and large city is the best antidote to the fragmentation and normal disunity that occurs in a city.

3. An effective network requires the participation of the "three-legged stool"—pastor, marketplace leader, and ministry leader.

A PRAYER

Jesus, we pray for our cities today. Like in Phoenix, you are drawing the nations of the world into our neighborhoods. Speak today into our cities through your united church. Amen.

26

Children

GORDON AND CAROL SCHRANK BRING AWANA TO RWANDA

All your children will be taught by the LORD, and
great will be their peace.

Isaiah 54:13

Isaiah writes about a future vision of children growing up in the fear and admonition of the Lord. Christian parents long for their children to carry on their spiritual legacy into future generations. How a society treats its children is its best measure of its humanity. The world is increasingly a dangerous place for children with large-scale poverty and misery everywhere. Agencies like Awana and leaders like Valerie Bell are addressing this reality.

Awana

Over the course of twenty years, I've been deeply impressed with Valerie. She is an exceptional communicator—both as a writer and speaker—but I have always seen her engagement with children from a distance, even though she was part of a World Vision trip to Africa with me in the early 2000s.

In 2016 Valerie was named CEO of Awana International. Awana began in 1950 and is a discipleship program that reaches children from age three through high school. It is highly relational, highly biblical, and highly fun. The program currently works among 3.74 million children in 117 nations. Forty-four thousand churches are involved, and one hundred denominations are represented. Awana has had one of the most enduring impacts on children. Because of many disruptive, generous partners like Gordon and Carol Schrank, Awana has grown rapidly, becoming the global leader in child discipleship.

I asked Valerie and Matt Markins, Awana's president, who they would nominate to tell a story of disruptive generosity. They nominated Gordon and Carol Schrank, and this is their story.

Faithful Roots

Gordon and Carol grew up in families who loved the Lord and valued church involvement. Carol says, "My parents were known for their faithfulness. They were faithful to each other, faithfully served their local church body, and were faithful in their giving. My dad was promoted to assistant fire chief for our Southern California community, and he had to occasionally work weekends.

"He got permission from our pastor to come dressed in his uniform and bring his radio along should he be called to a fire. My dad modeled that kind of faithfulness to the church. I noticed that my mom and dad gave every week in their contribution envelope. That taught me that regular giving was the right thing to do."

Carol made a faith commitment at the age of thirteen, when she attended a weekend retreat. She says, "I realized that I needed to accept Christ for myself. I was shaped by my involvement with Campus Crusade in college." Carol's involvement led her to Dallas to join Campus Crusade staff after graduation, where she was assigned to a singing group.

Gordon similarly grew up in a godly home in the Dallas area. His parents demonstrated the same kind of faithfulness Carol's did. He says, "I was involved in a local church and attended a parochial school through the sixth grade. My parents were always at church and active in its leadership. I always remember my dad pulling out that little white envelope every Sunday and placing it in the offering."

Gordon and Carol's lives intersected through Campus Crusade friends in Dallas. Gordon's life was forever changed when his brother was killed in an automobile accident. He saw twelve virtual strangers in his apartment building rallied around him. That time remade him spiritually. As the result of the interaction with the Campus Crusade singers and their families, Gordon realized he needed to respond to the person of Christ himself. He says, "After my brother's death, I realized that life really is a gift not to be taken lightly."

Rwanda Disrupted

The Schranks married in 1974 and began to call Midland, Texas, home in 1979. Gordon was owner-operator of the Chick-fil-A restaurant in Midland for thirty-three years. As their own children grew up, the whole family was involved and thus affected by Awana. As they traveled, the Schranks also became aware of the impact of Awana in foreign countries, especially in China.

In the mideighties Gordon and Carol's perspective on money was forever changed when they heard Larry Burkett present the simple truth that "God owns it all." That profound biblical statement revolutionized their view of money and possessions, and prompted them to get out of debt and begin to honor the Lord with "firstfruit giving."

In 2012 they saw a presentation on Awana's global impact, including the scope of work across Europe, Asia, and Africa. Having worked in Rwanda on several occasions, Gordon and Carol were saddened to see that Rwanda had zero Awana clubs! They asked what it would take to launch the work there. The Awana leadership described the level of investment, time it would take to translate materials into the Rwandan language, and the plan for training.

Having survived the 1994 genocide when one million people were killed in one hundred days, Rwanda has a globally significant story. I traveled there in 2003 and had two initial impressions. The first was the beauty of the country—it looked like Vermont to me, this land of a thousand hills. The second was that, with so much death in such a small country, Rwanda felt like a giant graveyard.

The Schranks agreed to make an initial investment for planting Awana in Rwanda. They told me, "We saw the opportunity to reach kids with the gospel of Christ. We had seen the eternal impact that Awana had on kids in our community and especially on our own children. And we also knew that the Awana organization was a good steward of their resources. We always ask the question, How much of our funding does the organization use to actually implement their strategy? We were really pleased with Awana's stewardship. We want our giving to be strategic and to accomplish as much as possible for the kingdom."

The Schranks were asked, "Why Rwanda?" They responded, "We had traveled to Rwanda with Chick-fil-A's WinShape

International program, and while there we fell in love with the beauty of the Rwandan people and their country. Because of the genocide, we knew that Rwandan children were resilient and even joyful." Gordon and Carol subsequently saw their own giving matched by the giving of others, including their own children.

The Schranks were told the initial translation of materials would take a year. To their surprise and delight, the translation and training were accomplished within the first year! The first report after the initial Awana training and launch saw 10,000 children involved. By 2015 the number had grown to 22,000, and by 2016 the number had more than doubled to 48,000 children participating in Awana programs that were less than three years old. It was God's movement.

As they reflected on the impact of their investment, the Schranks said, "We know that children are the most strategic age group to reach because most spiritual commitments are made by the age of fourteen. Already we have seen 320 Rwandan churches involved, and another 380 churches are receiving training in 2017." [1]

Isaiah and Children

Isaiah gave us the magnificent prophecy about the Christ child who will be born to a virgin. He will be the Everlasting Father, Prince of Peace, Mighty God, and Wonderful Counselor. Isaiah saw a day when children would be taught by the Lord, and that would bring peace.

POINTS TO CONSIDER

1. Faithfulness from one generation to the next can change the world.

2. God is the great multiplier of our generosity.

3. Reaching young children is a way to bring peace and healing to a country.

A PRAYER

*Jesus, you invited the little children to come to you.
Use the global church to reach the most vulnerable—
the masses of children now living in cities around
the world. Amen.*

27

Proclaim

TRAVIS SIMONE AND CLIFF BRIGHAM GET SERIOUS ABOUT GOSPEL MOVEMENTS

> I will set a sign among them, and I will send some of those who survive to the nations—to Tarshish, to the Libyans and Lydians . . . to Tubal and Greece, and to the distant islands that have not heard of my fame or seen my glory. They will proclaim my glory among the nations.
>
> Isaiah 66:19

The book of Isaiah concludes with a vision that God's people will go to the distant nations. As God's people do so, his glory will be proclaimed to these nations. What does that mean?

The glory of God in the gospel is that God the Son became a human being and lived the life we should have lived. He died the death we should have died. In his death, he put death to death. The beauty is that today the nations have come to our cities in the United States, such as Williamsburg, Virginia, where Travis Simone and Cliff Brigham lead.

Travis Simone

Travis Simone began attending Movement Day in New York City in 2012. He says, "I had begun to feel disconnected from the larger body of Christ. When I attended Movement Day I saw how leaders from churches in the same city felt deeply connected to one another. I was also deeply impacted by Tim Keller's teachings on gospel movements."

I was impressed with Travis. I believe the future of city gospel movements rests in the hands of younger leaders, particularly those between the ages of twenty-five and thirty-five. He stepped into a senior pastor role at the age of thirty-four at Williamsburg Community Chapel (WCC), a congregation with two thousand regular attendees. He is an initiator. He wrote a study guide companion for Tim Keller's book *Generous Justice*, and after Movement Day 2013 I introduced him to Keller, who was given a copy.

In the spring of 2016 Travis invited me to come to Williamsburg to meet with some of the community leaders. He wanted them to attend Movement Day Global Cities 2016 (MDGC). Travis had been bringing a team to New York City for Movement Day the past few years, and the goal was to broaden the team. One of the leaders who attended was Cliff Brigham, the chair of the elder board for WCC.

Travis has dedicated a year in the church's life to focus on the theme of God's movement. Travis started with God's first command to his people to be fruitful, multiply, and fill the earth (Genesis 1:28). He then looked at the movement of God's people throughout the Old Testament, the church as God's chosen vehicle for this movement, the movement of God toward humanity at Christmas, obstacles to the movement, prayer as a catalyst for movement, and ultimately how we are called to serve God's movement through the lens of the original gospel movement in the book of Acts.

Cliff Brigham

Cliff Brigham owns a CPA firm in the community. He had not planned to be at the luncheon, yet providentially he joined the conversation.

Cliff has roots in northern Virginia, dating back to his father's military career. He says, "Even though I attended church every Sunday growing up, I began to drift away in high school. I began to look to the occult in the mid-1960s. As I got more and more involved and realized the spiritual world was very real. What I didn't know was that I was heading in the wrong and dangerous direction."

God disrupted Cliff's life through a college roommate in his junior year. He recounts the experience. "I began to hear about the Jesus Movement in 1969 and 1970. I was drawn to it. My roommate was converted to Christ three days before we started rooming together. I was the second person he ever shared his faith with. I had to make some difficult decisions as the result of my new faith. I lost a lot of friends and a serious girlfriend, but I gained a whole new church family."

Cliff has led a full life with his tax practice and significant church involvements, and he has been active in missions with multiple trips to Africa. Cliff describes what God was stirring in him as the result of the luncheon. "I found that my vision and passion were identical to those being expressed about Movement Day. God captured my heart and imagination with what he was doing in cities all over the world. In the past several months, this vision has risen to represent one of my primary passions. One of the strengths of Movement Day is that it can go viral. Once it catches on, it will go around the world as the Holy Spirit burns the vision into the heart of his people, one person at a time."

Gospel Movement

In August 2016 Cliff and Travis invited me back to Williamsburg to share the vision of Movement Day with potential investors for scholarships. We were seeing an enormous need to assist African leaders. We had a dinner meeting in Cliff's home and a luncheon gathering at WCC.

On another Saturday I set up a conference call for leaders to meet Stephen Mbogo, the CEO of African Enterprise. Stephen was building a team of seventy Africans to attend Movement Day Global Cities. He said, "Movement Day is an incredibly important model for us in Africa. The church is growing rapidly in our cities, but we are so competitive with each other over Western resources."[1]

Cliff commented, "Movement Day has also captured my wallet. It has disrupted my plans. I see the opportunities that Movement Day has become to empower local and national leaders to bring unity and the kingdom into their cities. The possibilities are limitless. That is why I think this is so important. God is calling my wife and me out of our comfort zone. We have a chance to make an amazing difference and are committed 100 percent in on this. Supporting just one national leader to come to Movement Day can have consequences for decades to come."

Cliff made a significant contribution to assist Africans coming to MDGC. He told me after the conference, "The exact size of my contribution made to MDGC came back to me unexpectedly through a client. It was a remarkable way of God confirming his hand is on this effort."[2]

Travis is leading his congregation through a year of teaching on the theme of God's movement among his people in the Bible. He is teaching through the Gospels and the book of Acts and the ways the movement of God spread out into the world. The leaders of the church are reading through one of Keller's books on understanding movements.

Travis said, "We are serious about understanding what it means to see God create a movement. We are praying every Friday morning as a congregation toward this vision. We want to be a church of partnership instead of a church that just consumes programs. The aspiration in the next three to five years is that we will see citywide partnerships emerge. We don't want to just be a thumb dangling from the body of Christ. We want to see an authentic gospel movement from Williamsburg that will impact the world."[3]

Isaiah and the Gospel

The book of Isaiah ends with the promise that all the nations and lands will learn about the glory of God. We are seeing that come to fruition in our day with the rapid growth of the gospel in cities around the world.

POINTS TO CONSIDER

1. A gospel movement requires getting connected to the broader body of Christ.

2. Generosity of relationships can empower leaders from around the world.
3. Teaching and praying are important foundations for an explosive movement.

A PRAYER

Jesus, you came as the great sign of a movement that would extend to all people everywhere. Give us your determination to do our part in reaching the world with your message. Amen.

28

Abundance

EMILIE AND CRAIG EQUIP OTHERS TO EVANGELIZE

"To whom will you compare me? Or who is my equal?" says the Holy One. Lift up your eyes and look to the heavens: Who created all these? He who brings out the starry host one by one and calls forth each of them by name. Because of his great power and mighty strength, not one of them is missing.

Isaiah 40:25–26

Isaiah 40 helps us to see the enormity and the power of God. He is described as one who is supreme above every creation in the universe. In his omniscience, he knows everything. In his omnipresence, he is everywhere. In his abundance, he owns everything.

As a leader, I have been inspired by the Global Leadership Summit in its vision to help leaders become better. At the first GLS the idea of the New York City Leadership Center was conceived and brought to fruition in 2008. By 2010 we birthed Movement Day, which is now spreading to cities on all five continents. Movement Day has become a sister initiative to the Global Leadership Summit.

In an interview with Emilie from Florida, I discovered that the initial contribution to help plant the GLS in 1995 came in part from her family. Her father, Ed Prince, was an early supporter of Bill Hybels. In Western Michigan, which includes the city of Grand Rapids, an extraordinary community of philanthropists is changing the world.

Ed Prince began his career in the die-cast business in Holland, Michigan, and he later started his own manufacturing business. By the 1990s the company employed thousands of workers. His business success allowed the family to support several major spiritual and civic causes, and since 1983 the company has created a $1 million matching fund opportunity each year for employees and the company to give to local causes.

Prince died suddenly in 1995. Emilie commented, "My dad's death devastated us. Even though he has been gone for twenty years, his actions still impact the world today. Dad was an encouraging visionary, even though he was fully human."

From Grand Rapids to Florida

Emilie and her husband, Craig, now live in Florida. They own car dealerships as well as a yacht brokerage company, where they sell and lease yachts.

One of their philanthropic involvements is bringing the Global Leadership Summit to their region of Florida. Emilie came to the 2016 Movement Day Global Cities gathering in New York City, where she met hundreds of Christian senior marketplace leaders laboring to make an impact on their cities.

I am impressed by Emilie and Craig's engagement in an affluent community. She says, "We moved to an area where spiritual life was conducted at a chapel. The chapel had no Bibles. We found very few people of faith. Our greatest ministry in this community is offering our time—time to take people out to dinner, take people out on the boat, and time spent learning together God's purpose for each of us that make up the church."

Emilie's own life was transformed by her engagement with Bible Study Fellowship in Grand Rapids at the age of twenty-five. Even though she had grown up in the church, she didn't learn some of the truths of Scripture until that encounter through BSF.

She reflected on growing up in a high-profile family in a deeply churched community. "My father began his company in 1965. My siblings and I were four, six, and eight. It was a consuming experience. Growing up in West Michigan, we learned that you can do anything or be anything. You just have to work hard. We were surrounded by many innovators and entrepreneurs who grew large, successful businesses. Moving to Florida was a big change for Craig and me culturally and spiritually."

From Florida to the World

Emlie described philanthropic efforts her family has been involved with that span the generations. She said, "My parents went to Israel in 1993 and met a great Bible teacher. They traveled for my mom's sixtieth birthday. That trip changed my dad's life spiritually. He decided to financially underwrite That the World May Know. This became a DVD resource filmed in Israel.

Each of the fourteen faith lessons was twenty to thirty minutes long. Sessions were narrated by Ray Vander Laan. The Bible came alive to my dad in that trip, and millions have received a taste of his Israel experience through this series.

"We have continued that experience by taking people to Israel since 2002. It has provided an incredible discipleship and church-building experience. We are so excited every year for the opportunity to facilitate several people to have their first experience of Israel."

In addition to annual trips to Israel, the family has been involved with the Haggai Institute. Emilie and Craig have both served on its board. A mutual friend, Bev Upton, serves as its CEO, and the ministry is a Movement Day partner. Haggai Institute trains leaders to multiply their Christian witness in many of the hardest places on earth spiritually.

The Haggai Institute was founded in 1969 by John Haggai, the son of a New Englander and a Syrian immigrant. It has provided training to leaders in 110 countries over nearly fifty years, and the alumni of the Haggai Institute now number more than twenty-eight thousand. The exponential model of Haggai's training is seen in its vision to have every alumnus reach one hundred people in their context.

Emilie commented, "My family has traveled around the world twice with the Haggai Institute. When we traveled to India, I saw my ten-year-old weeping when he saw children living in the street. This international exposure has deeply shaped our family and forged our values."

Emilie commented on the principles that have guided their philanthropy. She said, "Generosity is about living abundantly in relationships. You can give away a lot of money but not be living abundantly. The Lord loves a cheerful giver, and that is what we strive to be in all of our life, whether it is taking a friend to Israel, writing a check, or baking a pie for a neighbor."[1]

Isaiah and God's Abundance

Isaiah pointed to a God who is cosmic in his nature, the absolute owner of everything in the universe. God is abundant. He wants us to grasp the meaning of our lives through the prism of his abundance and authority over all things.

POINTS TO CONSIDER

1. Abundance is rooted in a relationship with God and relationships with others.
2. Global travel is an important way to gain a perspective on God's work in the world.
3. Our giving today can affect generations to come and be highly leveraged to change the world.

A PRAYER

Jesus, you are the Abundant God who became poor that we might experience the ultimate abundance. May our lives and our generosity reflect this perspective that you modeled so generously for us. Amen.

29

Witness

JOHN MAISEL AND CHUCK ANDERSON TAKE A STAND FOR CHRIST

"You are my witnesses," declares the LORD, "and my servant whom I have chosen, so that you may know and believe me and understand that I am he."

Isaiah 43:10

Isaiah draws an important relationship between knowing the Lord and being a witness for the Lord. Witnessing our faith to others is perhaps the first great sign that we, in fact, do know the Lord. In our witness, we grow in our own understanding of who God is as the Ultimate Witness. John Maisel and Chuck Anderson have been vibrant witnesses in Dallas for decades.

John Maisel

John has been one of the common threads in my time in Dallas, connecting with dozens of common relationships. He is a Vietnam War veteran who earned a Bronze Star and Purple Heart after being wounded. He began traveling in the 1980s into communist countries to share the gospel behind the Iron Curtain. In 1993 he birthed East-West Ministries, a church planting and discipling movement active in nine global regions across Europe, Africa, Asia, and the Middle East. East-West is currently focused on a five-year vision to multiply one million new disciples in the spiritually darkest area of the world.

Chuck Anderson

Chuck had come to Dallas to attend Southern Methodist University and to play basketball in the early 1980s. Moving to Dallas was a new experience after playing basketball at the University of Nebraska for one year. Chuck says, "I met my wife, Kim, in Florida, and she also transferred to SMU. We dated for the next three and a half years before I graduated in 1984. We were married the next year."

Chuck began to work for Trammell Crow, a prestigious Dallas real-estate firm. In 1997 the company went public and he experienced a significant financial return for the investment he made in his career. Chuck commented on that experience. "I thought I had it all. I had a great family. I was in great shape. The senior executives decided to attend the Cooper Clinic for a rigorous physical. I was told that I was in the top 1 percent of the population regarding my health. I wanted to know if there were any more tests that I could take to be doubly sure everything had been evaluated. They did a CT scan."

During the CT scan a mass was found on Chuck's right kidney. The next day the prognosis was that it was 99 percent likely he had kidney cancer. He says, "I thought I was king of the world, but now with the test results I thought I might only have a few years to live. Fortunately, the cancer had not metastasized. The doctors took out the right kidney. I was thirty-seven years of age. It was a scary time."

After the surgery, Skip Ryan, then pastor at Park Cities Presbyterian Church in Dallas, met with Chuck. He asked him the question, "If you died and went to heaven and God asked you if he should let you in, what would you say?" Chuck responded, "I am a good person, a good father and husband." He later reflected that it was a weak answer.

In February 1998 Chuck began meeting in regular Bible study, with John Maisel. During the first few weeks of this study, the scales fell off Chuck's eyes and he had a defining moment of conversion to Christ. He says, "I wondered if I should leave real estate to become a missionary. Maisel talked me off the ledge and challenged me to use my marketplace platform. Over the past eighteen years, I have met with hundreds of young guys coming through Dallas to talk about the real-estate profession. I get to share my faith in Christ with them as well."

Chuck left Trammell Crow in 2002 to form a new firm, Bandera Ventures. His two partners have worked with him for over thirty years. Their real estate includes office buildings, industrial buildings, and data centers, all in the commercial space. Chuck says they have completed more than eighty projects.

Chuck's Ministries and John's Influence

The Andersons joined Watermark Community Church in 2003. Watermark is especially known for attracting and engaging millennial leaders. Chuck says, "What I like about Watermark is its call to high commitment. Every person renews their membership every year, and every member is active in a community group and serving at the church."

His involvement with Watermark, East-West Ministries, and YWAM (Youth with a Mission) have taken him to Cuba four times, Africa three times, and on home-build trips sixteen times with his family. The trips to Cuba hosted by East-West Ministries are a week of witnessing with Cuban national Christians. Typically, a team of men travel together and stay in Havana for a week. Ray Nixon takes a new group every year (see chapter 1).

Chuck commented on the influence of John Maisel on his life. "I have never been in a restaurant with John when he didn't initiate a conversation about spiritual things with a waiter or restaurant staff. He does it lovingly and winsomely. He has helped me to deepen my conviction that I want everyone who knows me to know what I believe."

Another East-West Ministries board member commented, "The impact of East-West under John Maisel's leadership has been transformative in countries like Cuba and India. I got to see with my own eyes the power of the gospel in very different places. It was transformative for me as well to share my faith with leaders. East-West is being used to train local leaders, plant churches, and transform cities with the gospel."[1]

Isaiah's Witness

Isaiah represented God in a country that was declining spiritually and morally. He called the nation back to a view of God that transcended history and their momentary challenges. The words of Isaiah have given us the best understanding of Jesus as Messiah in the Old Testament. Isaiah was perhaps the greatest witness to the coming of Christ in the Old Testament.

POINTS TO CONSIDER

1. God uses the crises of our lives to awaken our need for him.
2. God desires our greatest boldness to represent him in all places at all times.
3. Christian marketplace leaders have a unique platform to share their faith through the excellence of their professions.

A PRAYER

Jesus, give us your boldness as you spoke to those who opposed you and put you to death. Help us to realize the unique opportunities our professions have given us to be your voice. Amen.

30

Kings

CHRIS RENFER GOES BIG FOR THE GOSPEL

> The vision concerning Judah and Jerusalem that
> Isaiah son of Amoz saw during the reigns of Uz-
> ziah, Jotham, Ahaz and Hezekiah, kings of Judah.
>
> Isaiah 1:1

I made my first trip to Dubai in July 2015. It's a remarkable city in a remarkable region of the world. My first impressions of Dubai included the magnificent architecture, the enormous malls, and the diversity of the expat community. As many as 90 percent of those living in Dubai have immigrated.

The first meeting I attended there was hosted by Prem Nair, an Indian businessman. Prem took me to meet Chris Renfer, a businessman from Switzerland. Chris has been living in Dubai since 2010 in the capacity of group general manager for a major Middle East business group. His group is specialized in the technology business and civil engineering.

Chris and a mutual friend, Kevin Griffiths, from Emirates Airline, attended Movement Day Global Cities in New York City in October 2016. Chris says they came because they believe God can't steer a parked car, and they wanted to see what doors God may be opening for them through Movement Day as senior marketplace leaders. Chris confesses, "Being a Christian marketplace leader in the Middle East can be a very lonely experience. It was tremendous to meet other leaders who have a common heart for the world."

From the Alps to the Land of Kings

Chris grew up in middle-class Switzerland. His father was an accountant, then CFO of a production company. That business necessitated his traveling to Brazil, India, and Thailand. And at the age of fifty-two, his father started a consulting business. Chris got the travel bug from his dad as well as from a passion for the mountains.

He says, "My most remarkable memory about my father was hiking across the Alps. I learned how to have a childlike trust in my earthly father and also my heavenly Father. We hiked from north to south and east to west. I was completely dependent on my father's guidance."

Chris did his studies in economics and information technology before he joined an American IT company. He began to lead teams involved with systems integration and also worked for Siemens and Hewlett-Packard. A big opportunity came in 2007 when he accepted the chief of staff position for AIG Private Bank.

A big opportunity came in 2007 when he accepted the chief of staff position for a Swiss private bank. Chris spent a lot of the time in Southeast Asia and finally relocated to Dubai. I asked Chris why he thought this opportunity opened up for him. He said, "We received a prophecy from a stranger. He told us that I would serve the kings of the Mid East and my wife would touch women you usually cannot touch. This brought us to Dubai, and the prophecy became reality: my wife is working in the health care sector and has impressive encounters with local people. I have had the opportunity to meet several highly influential and very wealthy leaders in the Middle East. They are some of the best people I have met and some of the greatest world leaders that one could ever know."

Spiritual Journey

Chris was shaped by his family spiritually. He had health issues as a young adult, which caused him to learn to trust God for his well-being. Chris became active with the Vineyard Church and invested into the leadership development of church and marketplace leaders across Europe.

Chris expressed his spiritual commitment by helping to found the Praise Camp Movement in 1998 in Switzerland. The camp was designed for young people to encounter God through worship and Scripture. Chris says, "The camp was something new. We wanted to give God room to come into the lives of young people. We met every other year and hosted several thousand young people. It is the largest youth movement in Switzerland."

God challenged the camp movement team to "go big" in Switzerland. That first camp looked as though there would be only a few hundred participants—a financial disaster. Chris says, "God spoke to us and said, 'This is not your problem. Take what I give you and make the best of it.' At the end of the first camp was a a loss of several thousand Swiss francs. Five weeks later the camp had become profitable. I learned that what God is ordering, he is paying for."

Now 7,500 young people are attending the camp. The age range of participants is thirteen to twenty-five, and the attendees are predominately Swiss. I asked Chris about the impact of the camp. "We have young people who are confused about where they come from. Some have multiple fathers. One fourteen-year-old young woman was in the camp and had a powerful encounter with God. A few weeks later she died in a traffic accident, but she died with the assurance of both her heavenly Father and earthly father. Her father sent a note telling of the peace in her face and how grateful he was for the camp." Given the recent trajectory of Christianity in Europe, this is a remarkable story.

When I asked Chris about his principles of philanthropy, he told me, "My giving is not a formal process. I get an impression to invest. I have found that generosity leads to gratitude, which leads to worship, which leads to generosity. I want to live my life from a posture of worship, generosity, and gratitude. Generosity is always born from a place of love."

I invited Chris to share a memory of generosity. He said, "After we moved to Dubai we owned one last house in Zurich. I knew a family from Switzerland and living in New Zealand who felt called to go back to Zurich, and he had gotten a job as a teacher. My wife and I decided to give them the house we had left in Zurich to live in free for three years. They founded a church, we sold the house after three years, and the value of the house had a major financial gain. We saw that God guided us to let them live in the house for free, and we are now getting a great return and can invest again in another project. Just like God providing for the lady in 1 Kings 10 who ran out of food for her child, God can provide supernaturally. I like to call it God's Economy."[1]

Chris and I talked about the importance of marketplace Christians and their role in expanding the impact of the gospel.

He said it's important for leaders to confront themselves, to find their calling in their jobs, and to go for it.

Isaiah Served Kings

Isaiah was a leader who influenced national events by virtue of his relationship to four kings. He is a reminder to us all what a faithful confidant one can be to leaders of great national influence. The world needs more leaders like Isaiah who are God's voice in the halls of power.

POINTS TO CONSIDER

1. God can give favor between national leaders and marketplace leaders of faith.
2. God pays for what he orders.
3. Generosity leads to gratitude, which leads to worship, which leads to generosity.

A PRAYER

Jesus, you are the King of Kings. Warm the hearts of kings and presidents around the world toward you, marketplace leaders of faith, and toward your gospel. Amen.

31

Seeds

YUK LYNN WOO CHEN AND ROY CHEN
SEE THE BIBLE COME ALIVE

For as the soil makes the sprout come up and a
garden causes seeds to grow, so the Sovereign LORD
will make righteousness and praise spring up before
all nations.

Isaiah 61:11

Isaiah 61 introduces the text Jesus uses to make his inaugural
address in Luke 4 about the nature of his own coming. The
chapter is filled with joyful images. Cities are renewed, lives
are rebuilt, and great news is given to the poor. The seeds of
the gospel are sown and bear much fruit for the multitudes.

Generosity is sowing seed that bears much fruit all over the
world. Generosity is what makes the intangible tangible. Generosity is what sows the seeds of God's good news into bad
circumstances and produces a harvest of joy.

The director of the Ray Bakke Centre for Urban Transformation in Hong Kong, Natalie Chan, brought a team to Movement

Day Global Cities in New York City in 2016. She was building a team to bring about Movement Day Hong Kong. There Natalie introduced me to husband and wife Roy Chen and Yuk Lynn.

Seeds Foundation

The Chens have worked together at Grace Financial Limited since September 2008. They met in business school at Columbia University in New York City. Yuk Lynn is a third-generation family member involved in the fabric industry. In our interview, she told me, "My passion is for the transformation of societies through businesses that employ best practices in a sustainable and responsible manner."

The Chens have created the Seeds Foundation, a family-founded granting foundation with a mission of "seeding, cultivating and harvesting the capacity of individuals, communities and enterprises to enable sustainable social transformation."[1]

The Chens have deep spiritual roots. Yuk Lynn's family came from China in the late 1940s. She was taken to church in the United Kingdom and attended Redeemer Presbyterian Church in New York City. She was baptized in Los Angeles.

Roy is a third-generation Christian. His grandmother cultivated Christian belief in her five children and her grandchildren. The grandchildren all participated in Scripture memorization.

The Chens describe their philanthropic awakening journey in the following way: "The Si Yuan Foundation was founded by Roy's parents to give back to society. They wanted to inspire others to give. The foundation focused on educational needs in Hong Kong and China. The ZeShan Foundation was established in 2004 by Roy and his siblings. A focus was the elimination of hepatitis B. The Seeds Foundation was started in 2009. The purpose is to foster life transformation, community building, and spiritual formation."

Operation Wings of the Dove

One of their most recent projects was to sponsor 1,372 immigrants from Ethiopia during Operation Wings of the Dove, which brought Ethiopian Jews to Israel. Roy commented, "For us it has been like seeing the Bible come alive." The journey toward this sponsorship began in March 2005 when both Yuk Lynn and Roy had powerful encounters with the Lord, who began speaking to them about a shared passion. Their reading of Psalm 68 prompted them to pursue this sponsorship opportunity.

This journey led them to assist the Ethiopian Jews to settle in Israel. As prompted by the Lord, they used some of the proceeds from the sale of their home to make this possible, believing there were people in their community who needed financial assistance.

Ongoing Philanthropy

The Chens have been involved with a diverse number of projects: orphan care in China, church planting in the United States, training health professionals in North Korea, disaster relief in the Philippines and Myanmar, and health issues in Hong Kong. They have fully entered the discipline of hearing from God to guide their decision-making.

An important discipline the Chens have exercised in their philanthropy has been exercising due diligence for prospective grantees. They are careful to weigh the ability of the agency to steward the resources to be entrusted to them.

In 2006, Roy recounts, he was awakened at night after listening to Ed Silvoso, the Argentinian evangelist. He was challenged with the question, "Will you give 51 percent?" He and Yuk Lynn have worked very hard at listening to the Lord together during each stage of their marriage.

As we talked, the couple described a period in their marriage when working together was difficult. In 2011 they decided to repurpose their marriage and create a brand-new start. In 2012, with a hundred other couples at St. Andrews Church, they had a second wedding. They said the fruit of that renewed commitment was that they now celebrate each other.[2]

Isaiah and Sowing Seeds

In chapter 61 Isaiah described a partnership between the Sovereign Lord and the seed sower. This partnership results in great joy throughout the earth because as people who love the Lord listen to him, gospel seed gets strategically sown all over the planet.

POINTS TO CONSIDER

1. God uses generations of faithful Christian witnesses to expand the spiritual influence of the next generation.
2. Listening to God is an important discipline as one makes strategic philanthropic decisions.
3. Christian couples surrendered to each other and who celebrate each other have a powerful influence on the world.

A PRAYER

Jesus, you are the Great Seed Sower. Sow the seeds of our obedience and generosity to bear fruit in the hard places on the planet. Amen.

Afterword

John Rinehart's book *Gospel Patrons* draws the reader into the lives of men and women who wisely used their resources to advance the gospel message in the world. The model for saints to follow is illustrated by the first-century patrons who helped support the ministries of Jesus and Paul. God chooses to support the extension of the gospel message with help from men and women who love him! The first century saw the gospel flourish and lives transformed by the "patrons" of God's ministries.

One of the patron stories that most made an impact on me concerned a wealthy merchant, Humphrey Monmouth, who through his financial resources helped William Tyndale translate the Bible into English. Monmouth not only also financed printing the Bible but used his ships to deliver Bibles to other countries. Often, we believe our resources and abilities may not be enough to accomplish God's purpose, but this story shows one man—one patron—can make a world of difference! While we may not have the resources of a wealthy merchant, the story does encourage us to use our gifts to expand God's kingdom (Matt. 28:19).

I have shared *Gospel Patrons* with dozens of individuals. At a conference for East-West Ministries, where I serve as a board member, we gave the book to one hundred leaders. Most of the recipients had never thought of the concept of being a gospel patron. I love the idea that this simple two-word phrase—*gospel patron*—spells out exactly what we can become with our generosity. One person's support of William Tyndale changed world history forever. I intend to share this book at other ministry events in 2017, hopefully making an impression on their participants, as it has on me.

What I love about *A Disruptive Generosity* is that it provides us with modern-day gospel patrons. Mac Pier and I have talked about the themes of *Gospel Patrons* for two years. I am impressed that these principles that have expanded the influence of the gospel around the world in the past few centuries are now taking deep root in Africa, India, Europe, Korea, Singapore, the Caribbean, and North America.

Dallas Christian leaders who are deeply engaged have encouraged me in my walk with Christ for two decades. I have met several of the leaders featured in this book. I introduced Chuck Anderson to Mac Pier, and I am deeply encouraged by Chuck's story and his passion to share the gospel at every opportunity. Another influential leader whose story is in this book is John Maisel. John is a modern-day saint who encouraged me to travel to Cuba and share the gospel door-to-door for the last six years. His love and work for the Lord is contagious and inspiring. As you read these stories, you will see that the greatest joy in philanthropy is to be able to witness changed lives, communities, and cities.

Today we are in an information age when the truth has never been more silent. Psalm 105 says to "proclaim [the LORD's] name; make known among the nations what he has done." How do we awaken a culture to Jesus? What do we need to do to revive the nation? Millennials now outnumber baby boomers, and I believe they are the least churched and most biblically illiterate generation ever.

The Word of God, however, is what brings people to Jesus, not our voices. Our jobs are to lighten the load of those men and women who are on the front lines for Christ. How do we accomplish this? By understanding that God blessed all of us with resources to advance his kingdom. When we are generous gospel patrons, God allows us to participate and witness transformed lives.

My prayer is that *A Disruptive Generosity* will accelerate the movement of radical Christian philanthropy to reach the world with the gospel. Every movement needs to be fueled by a community journeying together in generosity.

Ray Nixon

Notes

Chapter 1 Boldness

1. Our Story, Serve West Dallas, http://www.servewestdallas.org/about/our-story/, accessed December 16, 2016.

2. Interview with Ray and Denise Nixon, Dallas, TX, December 16, 2016.

Chapter 2 Bound Together

1. John Stott, *The Lausanne Covenant*, https://www.lausanne.org/content/covenant/lausanne-covenant, August 1, 1974.

2. Interview with Terry Douglass and Doug Birdsall, Knoxville, TN, and Boston, MA, November 18, 2016.

3. Ibid.

Chapter 3 Game Changer

1. Interview with Priyan Fernando, Manhattan, NY, August 18, 2011.

2. Interview with Leslie Doll, Princeton, NJ, December 5, 2016.

3. Interview with Bob and Leslie Doll, Princeton, NJ, November 21, 2016.

Chapter 4 Glory

1. Interview with Ram and Sunita Gidoomal, London, November 30, 2016.

Chapter 5 illumiNations

1. Sam Roberts, "Listening to (and Saving) the World's Languages," http://www.nytimes.com/2010/04/29/nyregion/29lost.html, April 29, 2010.

2. John Rinehart, *This Book Is Alive*—an interview with Mart Green, March 31, 2016, http://www.gospelpatrons.org/films/this-book-is-alive.

3. Interview with Mart Green, Oklahoma City, OK, November 21, 2016.

Chapter 6 Light

1. Interview with Santosh Shetty, Dubai, November 15, 2016.

Chapter 7 Salvation

1. European Great Commission Coalition, http://egcc.eu/.
2. Interview with Adam Walach, Prague, November 15, 2016.

Chapter 8 Refuge

1. Joel Kotkin, "The World's Most Influential Cities," forbes.com, https://www.forbes.com/sites/joelkotkin/2014/08/14/the-most-influential-cities-in-the-world/#6c94bea47ad0, August 14, 2014.
2. Interview with Keith Chua, Singapore, November 20, 2016.

Chapter 9 Nations

1. Lausanne Cape Town Congress, Cape Town, South Africa, https://www.youtube.com/watch?v=0KEFbo2tJ_8, October 2016.
2. Interview with Sam Ko, Seoul, November 22, 2016.
3. Interview with Sunki Bang, Seoul, November 22, 2016.

Chapter 10 Harvest

1. Interview with Doug Birdsall, Boston, December 2, 2016.
2. Debora Vrana, "Developer's New Goal: Build Faith," http://articles.latimes.com/1994-10-09/business/fi-48482_1_missionary-work/2, October 9, 1994.
3. Ibid.
4. First Fruit Foundation, http://www.firstfruit.org/about-us/, accessed December 15, 2016.
5. Ibid.
6. Interview with Peter and Gail Ochs, Newport Beach, January 3, 2017.

Chapter 11 Word

1. Interview with DG Elmore, Indianapolis, IN, June 10, 2016.

Chapter 12 Friendship

1. Raymond H. Harris, *Anatomy of a Successful Firm,* 2008, self-published (available on Amazon, https://www.amazon.com/gp/offer-listing/B003163WN2).
2. *Architectual Record,* April 2015.
3. Raymond H. Harris, *The Heart of Business* (Colorado Springs: NavPress, 2013).
4. Interview with Raymond and Marydel Harris, Dallas, December 15, 2016.

Chapter 13 Joy

1. Interview with Scott Wittman, Mountain View, CA, November 18, 2016.

Chapter 14 Rebuild

1. Interview with Phil and Melissa Shaffer, Columbus, OH, November 16, 2016.

Chapter 15 Fruitful

1. Interview with Lewis Bakes, New Canaan, CT, November 21, 2016.
2. Interview with Tony Lembke, Springfield, NJ, December 1, 2016.

Chapter 16 Faithfulness

1. Interview with the Balmer family, Telford, PA, December 11, 2016.

Chapter 17 Vision

1. Interview with Zach Carlile, March 15, 2016, Dallas.

Chapter 18 Holding Fast

1. Interview with Graham Power, Cape Town, South Africa, November 20, 2016.

Chapter 19 Nobility

1. Interview with Darin and Paula Owen, Durban, South Africa, November 12, 2016.

Chapter 20 Spending Yourselves

1. Interview with Hannes van Aswegan, Pretoria, South Africa, November 22, 2016.
2. Ashburton Investments, LinkedIn, https://www.linkedin.com/company-beta/830071?pathWildcard=830071, accessed December 13, 2016.
3. Interview with Boshoff Grobler, Pretoria, South Africa, November 23, 2016.

Chapter 21 Good News

1. Christian Vision website, https://cvglobal.co/, accessed December 8, 2016.
2. Robert Watts, "Praise the Lord, I'm a Billionaire," http://www.thetimes.co.uk/article/praise-the-lord-im-a-billionaire-0hsnk8kzn, September 18, 2016.
3. Interview with Bob and Tracie Edmiston, Portugal, November, 21, 2016.

Chapter 22 Gospel

1. Interview with Wayne "Junior" Huizinga Jr. and Wayne Cotton, West Palm Beach, FL, May 2, 2016.

Chapter 23 Justice

1. Interview with Claude Alexander, National Discussion on Race, Manhattan, NY, October 24, 2016.

2. Interview with Don Gately, Charlotte, NC, November 23, 2016.
3. Interview with Ivan Hinrichs, Charlotte, NC, November 21, 2016.

Chapter 24 Praying

1. Jamaica Broilers mission statement, http://www.jamaicabroilersgroup.com/resources/corporate-data/mission-statement, accessed December 9, 2016.
2. Interview with Robert Levy, Kingston, Jamaica, November 14, 2016.

Chapter 25 Rising Sun

1. One Institute mission statement, http://oneinstitute.com/tile/about/.
2. Brad and Bret Edson, Marketplace One, http://leadershipx.squarespace.com/history/, accessed December 12, 2016.
3. Interview with Dale Marr, Tucson, AZ, November 22, 2016.

Chapter 26 Children

1. Interview with Gordon and Carol Shrank, Tirana, Albania, November 30, 2016.

Chapter 27 Proclaim

1. Interview with Stephen Mbogo, New York, October 25, 2016.
2. Interview with Cliff Brigham, Williamsburg, VA, November 15, 2016.
3. Interview with Travis Simone, Williamsburg, VA, November 22, 2016.

Chapter 28 Abundance

1. Interview with Emilie, Key Largo, FL, November 15, 2016.

Chapter 29 Witness

1. Interview with Chuck Anderson, Dallas, November 28, 2016.

Chapter 30 Kings

1. Interview with Chris Renfer, Dubai, November 9, 2016.

Chapter 31 Seeds

1. Seeds Foundation, http://www.seedsfoundationhk.com/.
2. Interview with Yuk Lynn and Roy Chen, Hong Kong, January 15, 2017.

Mac Pier is the founder and CEO of The New York City Leadership Center and was instrumental in founding the inaugural Movement Day conference. A resident of New York City since 1984, Mac lives in a diverse neighborhood with residents from more than one hundred ethnicities and attends church with people who speak sixty different languages. He is the author of *A Disruptive Gospel*, *Spiritual Leadership in the Global City*, and *Consequential Leadership*; coauthor of *The Power of a City at Prayer*; and a contributor to *Signs of Hope in the City*.

ALSO AVAILABLE FROM
MAC PIER

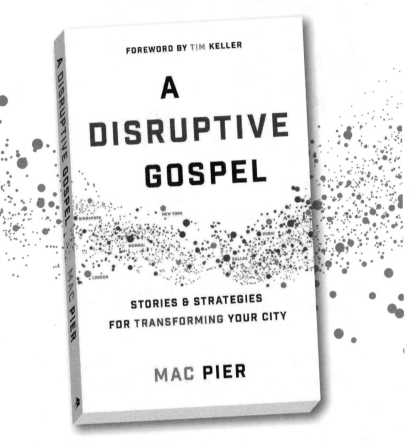

Mac Pier knows from firsthand experience that when the gospel invades your city, big things start to happen. For thirty years he's watched and participated in what God has been doing in New York City. In *A Disruptive Gospel*, he uncovers the greatest barriers to the gospel in major cities all over the world, shares hopeful stories of reconciliation, highlights the passion and leadership of young people advancing the gospel, and offers insight into how to start or join a gospel movement—wherever in the world you find yourself.

LIKE THIS BOOK?

Consider sharing it with others!

- Share or mention the book on your social media platforms. Use the hashtag **#DisruptiveGenerosity**.

- Write a book review on your blog or on a retailer site.

- Pick up a copy for friends, family, or strangers— anyone who you think would enjoy and be challenged by its message!

- Share this message on Twitter or Facebook: **I loved #DisruptiveGenerosity by @Movementday // @ReadBakerBooks**

- Recommend this book for your church, workplace, book club, or class.

- Follow Baker Books on social media and tell us what you like.

 Facebook.com/ReadBakerBooks

 @ReadBakerBooks